AA

·GLOVEBOX ATLAS·

BRITAIN

CONTENTS

Map symbols, Map pages
3

Road Maps
4-67

Ireland and Index
68-79

Index to placenames
80-96

2nd edition October 1992
Reprinted 1992
Reprinted with amendments April 1991
1st edition May 1990

© The Automobile Association 1992

Produced by the Publishing Division of The Automobile Association

Mapping produced by the Cartographic Department of The Automobile Association. This atlas has been compiled and produced from the Automaps database utilising electronic and computer technology.

Published by the Publishing Division of The Automobile Association, Fanum House, Basingstoke, Hampshire RG21 2EA.
ISBN 0 7495 0614 8, ISBN 0 7495 0615 6

Printed in Great Britain by BPCC Hazell Books, Paulton and Aylesbury

The contents of this atlas are believed correct at the time of printing, although the publishers cannot accept any responsibility for errors or omissions, or for changes in the details given. They would welcome information to help keep this atlas up to date; please write to the Cartographic Editor, Publishing Division, The Automobile Association, Fanum House, Basingstoke, Hampshire RG21 2EA.

A CIP catalogue record for this book is available from the British Library.

Map symbols

3

Atlas scale 1:500,000

0 — 5 — 10 mls
0 — 5 — 10 — 15 kms

8 miles to 1 inch

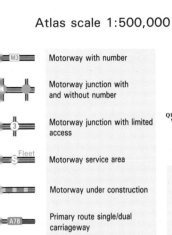

M3	Motorway with number
	Motorway junction with and without number
3	Motorway junction with limited access
Fleet / S	Motorway service area
	Motorway under construction
A78	Primary route single/dual carriageway
S	Primary route service area
A70	Other A road single/dual carriageway
B7078	B road single/dual carriageway
	Unclassified road, single/dual carriageway
	Road under construction
	Narrow primary, other A or B road with passing places (Scotland)
TOLL	Road toll
3 / M2 / 7	Distance in miles between symbols
— V —	Vehicle ferry - Great Britain
V BERGEN	Vehicle ferry - Continental
H CALAIS	Hovercraft ferry
	National boundary
	County boundary
PENZANCE H	Heliport
HEATHROW LONDON +	Airport

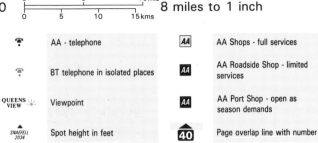

☎	AA - telephone
☎	BT telephone in isolated places
QUEENS VIEW	Viewpoint
SNAEFELL 2034	Spot height in feet
AA	AA Shops - full services
AA	AA Roadside Shop - limited services
AA	AA Port Shop - open as season demands
40	Page overlap line with number

Map pages

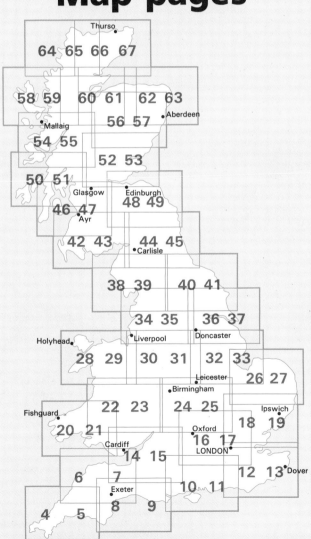

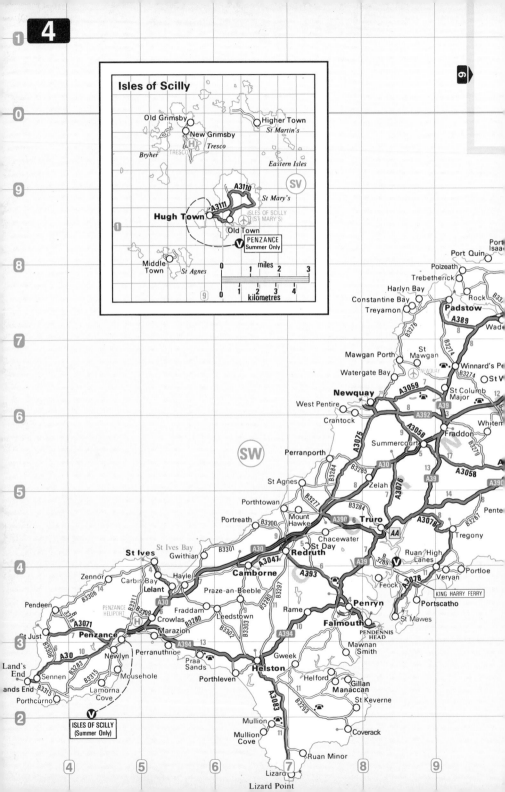

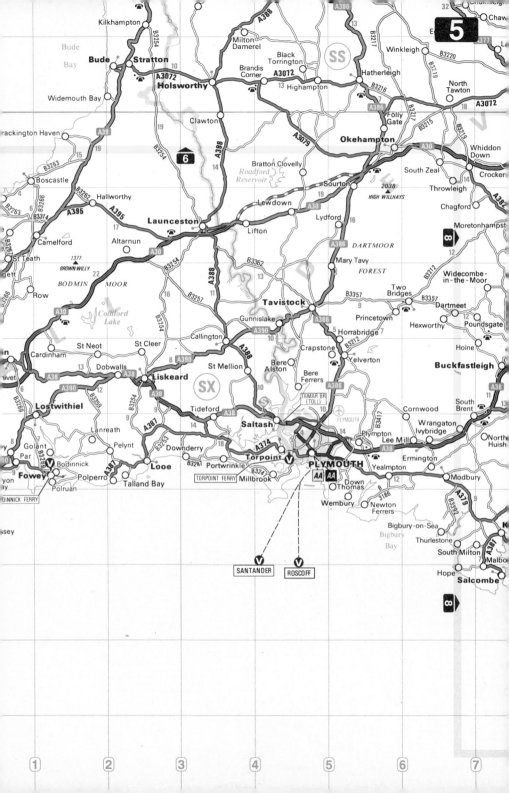

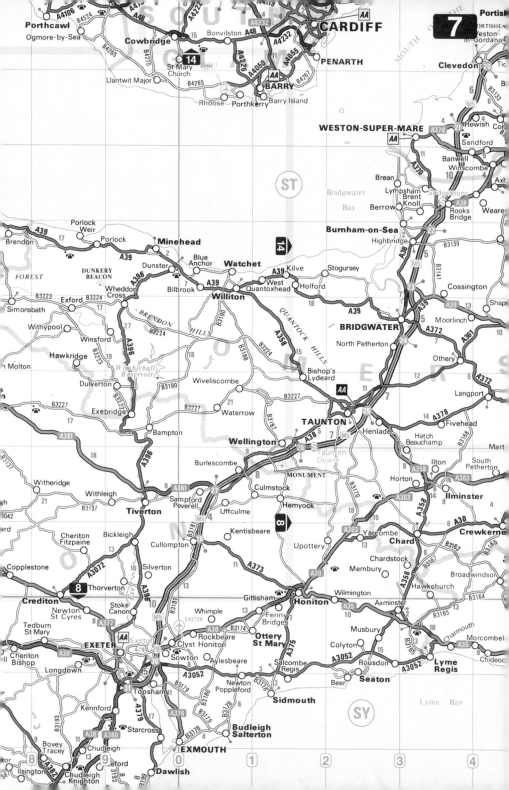

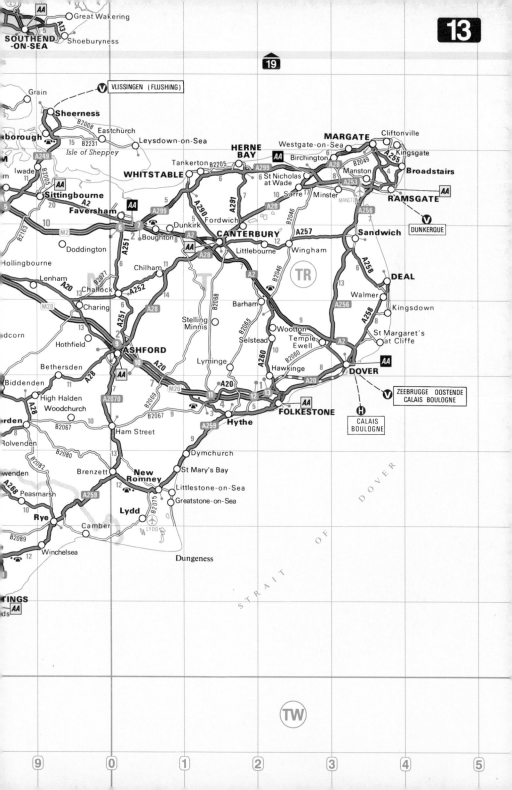

19

Great Wakering

SOUTHEND -ON-SEA

A13

Shoeburyness

VLISSINGEN (FLUSHING)

Grain

Sheerness

B2008

Eastchurch

Leysdown-on-Sea

borough

15 B2231

Isle of Sheppey

A249

MARGATE

Cliftonville

Westgate-on-Sea

Kingsgate

Birchington

A255

HERNE BAY

A28

B2049

Tankerton

B2205

A299

Manston

Broadstairs

WHITSTABLE

St Nicholas at Wade

A253

Iwade

B2005

Sarre

Minster

RAMSGATE

Sittingbourne

A2

5

A291

A28

MANSTON

A256

Faversham

A299

A290

B2046

DUNKERQUE

10

M2

6

Dunkirk

Fordwich

A257

Doddington

2

Boughton

A2

CANTERBURY

Sandwich

Hollingbourne

Littlebourne

Wingham

A258

Lenham

B2077

Chilham

TR

DEAL

A20

13

Challock

A252

14

Walmer

A256

Charing

A28

Barham

A258

Kingsdown

dcorn

A251

6

B2068

St Margaret's at Cliffe

Hothfield

Stelling Minnis

B2065

Wootton

A2

ASHFORD

Selstead

Temple Ewell

B2060

DOVER

Bethersden

A20

Lyminge

A260

Hawkinge

A20

Biddenden

A28

M20

A20

ZEEBRUGGE OOSTENDE CALAIS BOULOGNE

High Halden

A2070

11

FOLKESTONE

CALAIS BOULOGNE

Woodchurch

B2069

den

B2067

B2067

A259

Hythe

Ham Street

Rolvenden

B2080

13

Dymchurch

B2082

Brenzett

St Mary's Bay

wenden

New Romney

A268 Peasmarsh

A259

Littlestone-on-Sea

Greatstone-on-Sea

Rye

Lydd

B2075

LYDD

Camber

B2089

Winchelsea

Dungeness

STRAIT OF DOVER

TINGS

TW

9   0   1   2   3   4   5

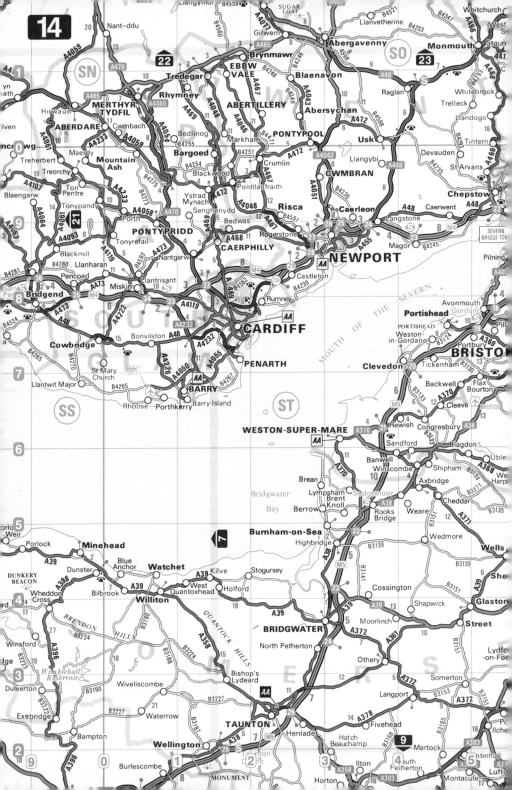

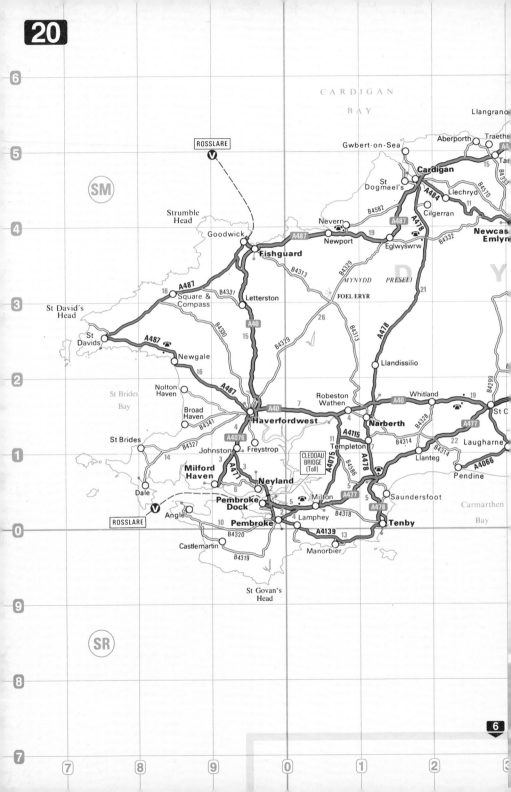

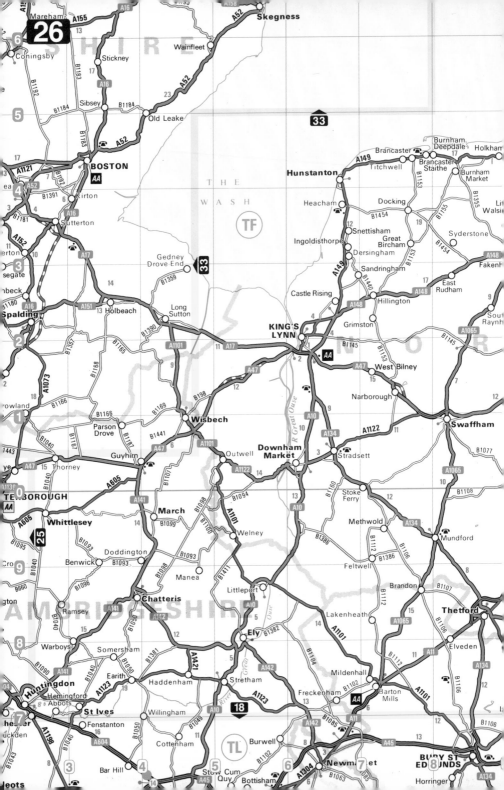

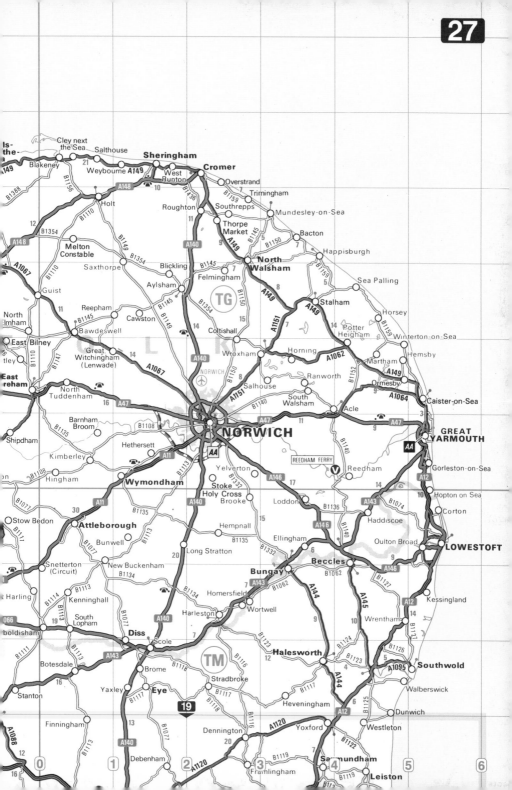

Cemaes Bay

Amlwch

A5025

17

B5111

DUBLIN
DUN LAOGHAIRE

Llanfaethlu

A5025

Llanerchymedd

Marianglas

GT ORMES

Benllech Bay

SOUTH
STACK

Holyhead

Llanfachraeth

B5112

B5109

19

Red Wharf Bay

Llangoed

Llandudno Jc

Penmaenmawr   Co

Trearddur Bay

Valley

A5

Four-Mile
Bridge

B5111

B5110

21

B5109

B5420

Beaumaris

Llanfairfec

Rower

Rhosneigr

A4080

10

18

B5109

Llangefni

Menai Bridge

A545

A5025

B5109

A5

Bangor

18 A55

Tal-y-Bo

Llanfair P.G.

A4080

7

8

Bethesda

Aberffraw

21

B4421/B4419

A4080

Port
Dinorwic

B4366

B4547

B4409

CARNEDD LLEWELYN
3484

Tre

Newborough

B4421

Caernarfon

Caeathro

Cwm-y-Glo

A5

16

Lla

SH

Llanwnda

Llanberis

A4086

Pen-y-
gwryd

A5

Capel

Caernarfon
Bay

Groeslon

13

18

A4086

Betws-y

B4418

SNOWDON
3560

Pen-y-groes

Rhyd-ddu

A498

Dolwyddelan

12

Clynnogfawr

A499

A4085

Trefor

Llanaelhaearn

19

Garn-
Dolbenmaen

Beddgelert

A498

16

Blaena
Ffestin

20

B4417

21

A499

PENINSULA

B4411

Prenteg

A487

Llanfrothen

A496

Ffestini

Nefyn

Tremadog

7

A487

4

Morfa-
Nefyn

A497

LLEYN

13

A497

Criccieth

Porthmadog

TOLL

Penrhyndeudraeth 5

A4212

14

B4417

7

Talsarnau

Trawsfy

Sarn

B4415

Llanbedrog

Pwllheli

TOLL

A496

A470

17

B4413

A499

Harlech

B4573

Y Rhiw

Abersoch

Llanbedr

13

Aberdaron

11

Ganll

*Bardsey
Island*

Dyffryn Ardudwy

Bontddu

A496

10

TOLL

Barmouth

Dolgella

Fairbourne

A493

20

A4

Llwyngwril

Tal-y-llyn

Corris

22

A493

19

B4405

Tywyn

Pennal

n by the Sea

otton
Easingston Staithes
cus
16
B1266 **A174** Sandsend
B1366
21
A171 **Whitby**
Ruswarp
Egton
Robin Hood's
Grosmont Bay
Goathland
Ravenscar
M O O R S
20
Rosedale Abbey **A171**
20 Cloughton
Lastingham
Hackness **Scalby**
Appleton-Le-Moors
Wrelton **SCARBOROUGH**
13 **A170** **A170** *AA*
Pickering East Ayton Eastfield
Thornton Wykeham 7
Dale 17 Seamer
Kirby Snainton **A64** **Filey**
Misperton **A1039**
8 Sherburn Staxton 7
B1258 Hunmanby **A165**
gham Reighton
B1257 Rillington 16
19 11 B1229
Malton B1249 Flamborough
A64 Head
18 B1248 Flamborough
North B1255
Grimston Rudston B1253
Whitwell Sledmere **A166**
on-the-Hill B1253 14 **BRIDLINGTON**
18 B1249
12 **A165** *(TA)*
Fridaythorpe Burton **A166**
A166 Agnes
29 **Great**
Stamford **Driffield** 16 15
Bridge **A163** **37** Skipsea
B1248 B1249
Bainton Beeford
A1079 B1246 **A164** B1241
Barmby B1248
Moor Pocklington Middleton on 13 **A165** **Hornsea**
18 the Wolds
15
B1248 B1244
Shiptonthorpe **A163** Leven
Market **A1035** B1243
Weighton **A1079** B1242
12
Holme upon **8** **9** **0** **Beverley** **1** **2** rough **3**
Spalding Moo A1034
19 Walkington **A1174**
vith **A163** B1230
H U M B E R S I D E

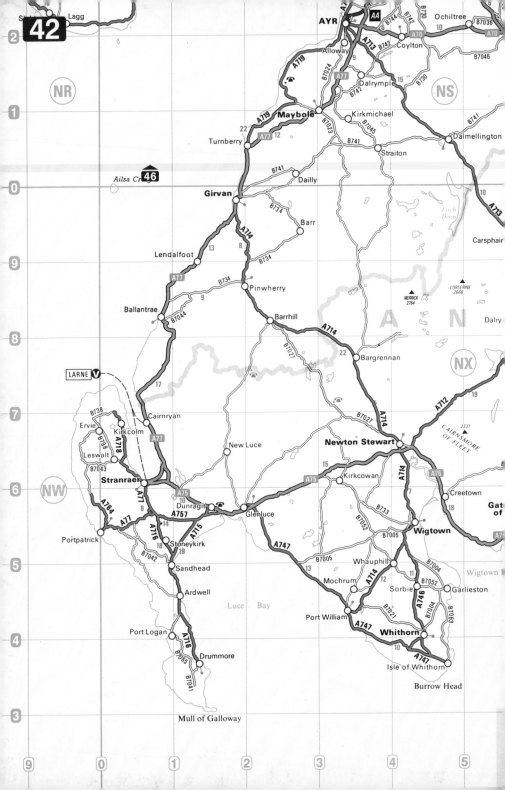

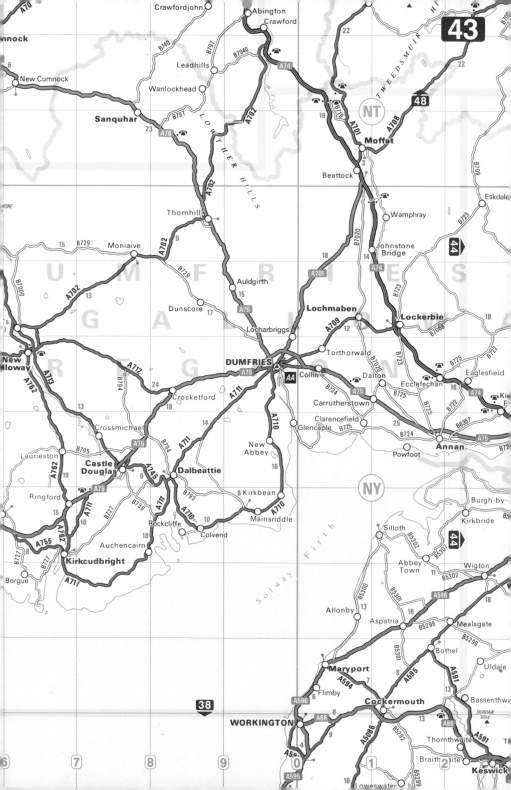

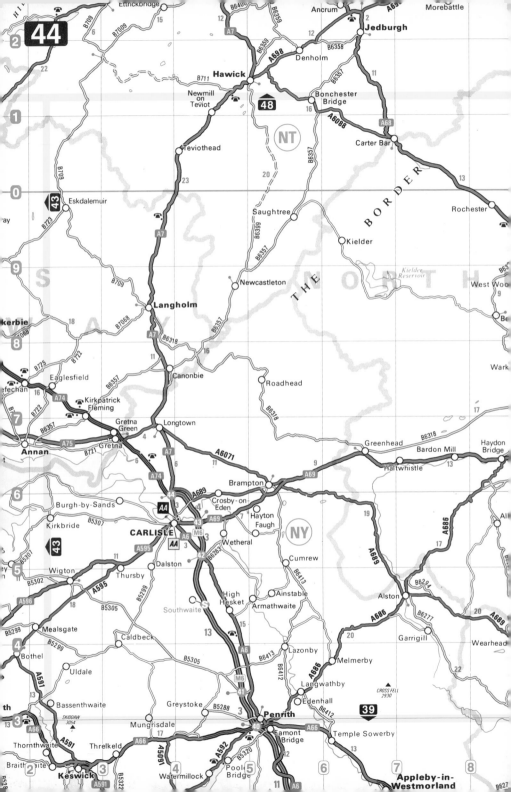

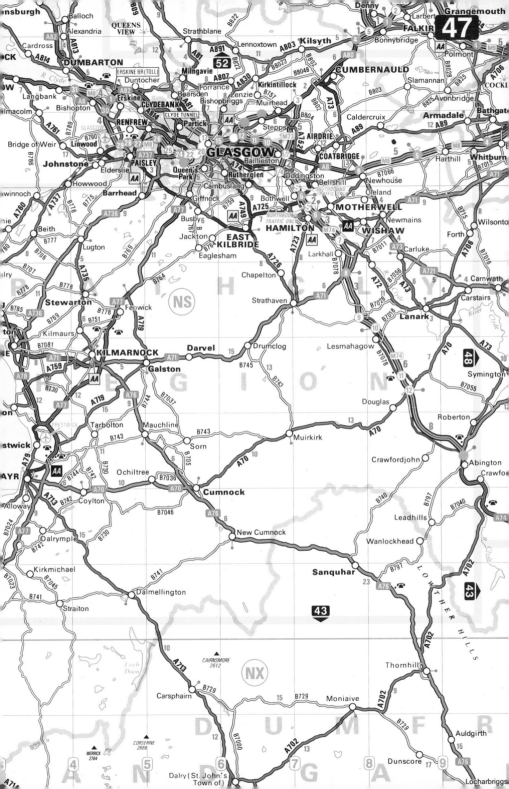

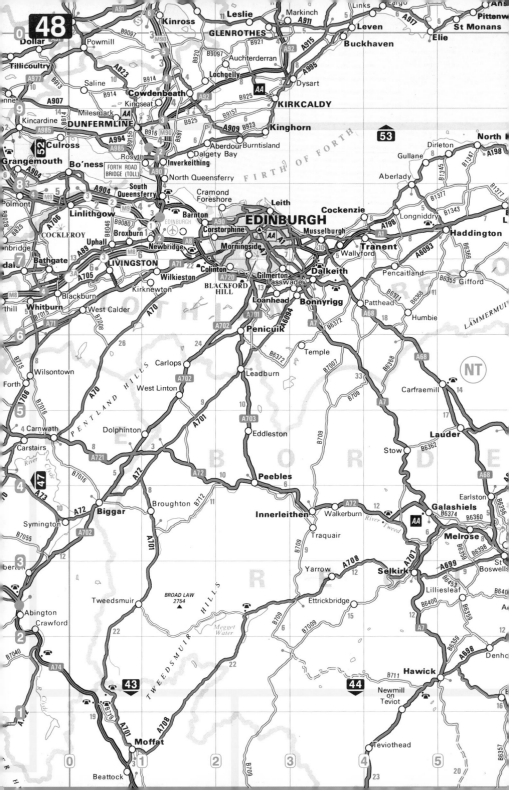

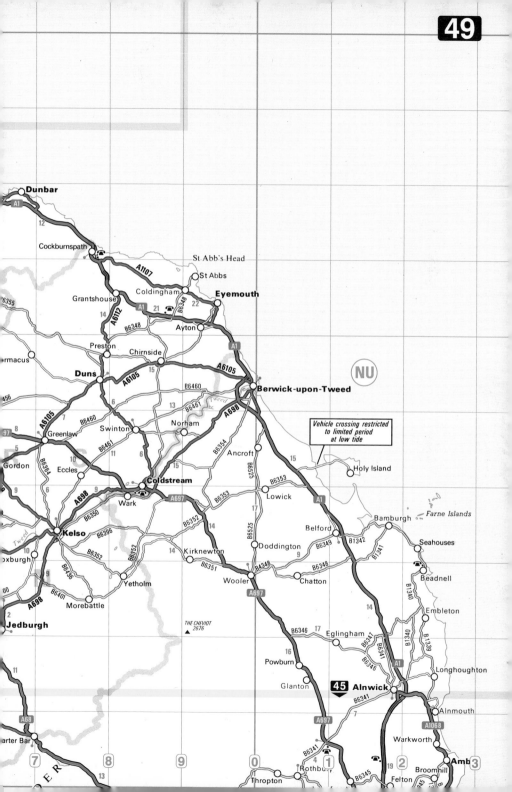

Dunbar

A1

12

Cockburnspath

A1107

St Abb's Head

St Abbs

Grantshouse

Coldingham

Eyemouth

A6112

A1 21

B6348 22

14

B6348

Ayton

Preston

Chirnside

rmacus

Duns

A6105

15

A6105

B6460

Berwick-upon-Tweed

NU

6355

B6355

456

A6105

7

B6460

6

13

B6461

Tweed

A698

97

8

Greenlaw

Swinton

Norham

B6354

Ancroft

15

Vehicle crossing restricted
to limited period
at low tide

Holy Island

Gordon

B6361

Eccles

10

B6461

11

6

15

B6525

Coldstream

Wark

A697

B6353

B6353

Lowick

A1

Farne Islands

9

6

A698

B6350

B6396

17

Bamburgh

Kelso

B6352

B6352

B6396

B6351

14

B6525

Doddington

Belford

B6349

B1342

Seahouses

oxburgh

10

B6436

Kirknewton

B4348

9

B6348

B1341

Beadnell

9

A698

B6401

Yetholm

Wooler

Chatton

B1340

Morebattle

A697

14

Embleton

2

Jedburgh

THE CHEVIOT
2676

B6346

17

Eglingham

B6347

B6341

B1339

11

16

Powburn

B6346

A1

Longhoughton

Glanton

45 Alnwick

Alnmouth

A68

A697

B6341

A1068

rter Bar

7

8

9

0

1

Warkworth

2

Amb 3

ER

13

B6341

Rothbury

19

Broomhill

Thropton

Felton

B6345

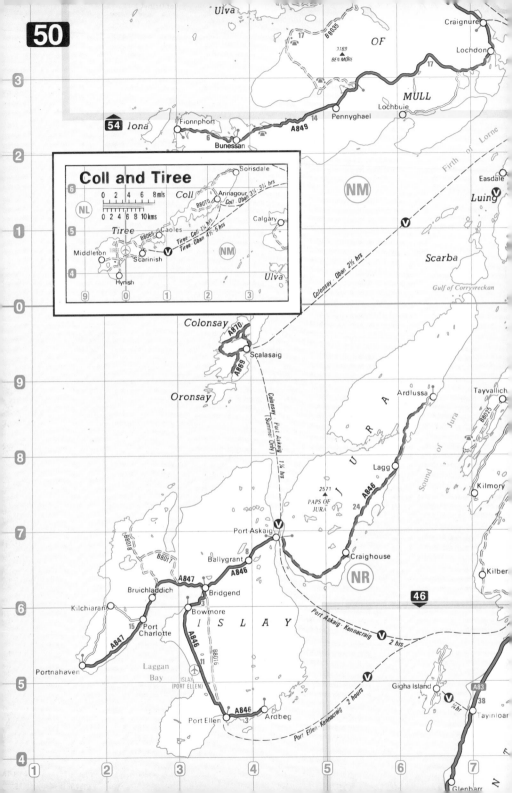

Ulva

OF

B8035

17

3169
BEN MORE

MULL

Craignure

Lochdon

17

Lochbuie

54 Iona

Fionnphort

Pennyghael

A849

14

6

Bunessan

Firth of Lorne

Easdale

Luing

NM

V

V

Scarba

Gulf of Corryvreckan

Coll and Tiree

Sorisdale

Coll

Arinagour

B8070

Coll-Oban 3¾ hrs

Coll Oban 1¾ hrs

NL

Calgary

0 2 4 6 8 mls

0 2 4 6 8 10 kms

Tiree

Caoles

B8069

Tiree-Coll 1¼ hrs

Tiree-Oban 4½–5 hrs

Middleton

TIREE

Scarinish

V

NM

Hynish

Ulva

9   0   1   2   3

Colonsay

Colonsay Oban 2¾ hrs

A870

Scalasaig

A869

Oronsay

Colonsay Port Askaig (Summer Only) 1¾ hrs

J   U   R   A

Ardlussa

Tayvallich

B8025

Sound of Jura

Kilmory

2571
PAPS OF
JURA

Lagg

24

A846

Port Askaig

V

Kilber

Ballygrant

8

Craighouse

NR

B8018

B8017

A847

A846

Bridgend

46

Bruichladdich

Port Askaig - Kennacraig

V 2 hrs

Kilchiaran

Bowmore

I S L A Y

Portnahaven

15

Port
Charlotte

A847

A846

B8016

V

Gigha Island

Port Ellen - Kennacraig 2 hours

V ¾ hr

A83

38

Tayinloan

Laggan
Bay

11

ISLAY
(PORT ELLEN)

Port Ellen

A846

3

Ardbeg

Glenbarr

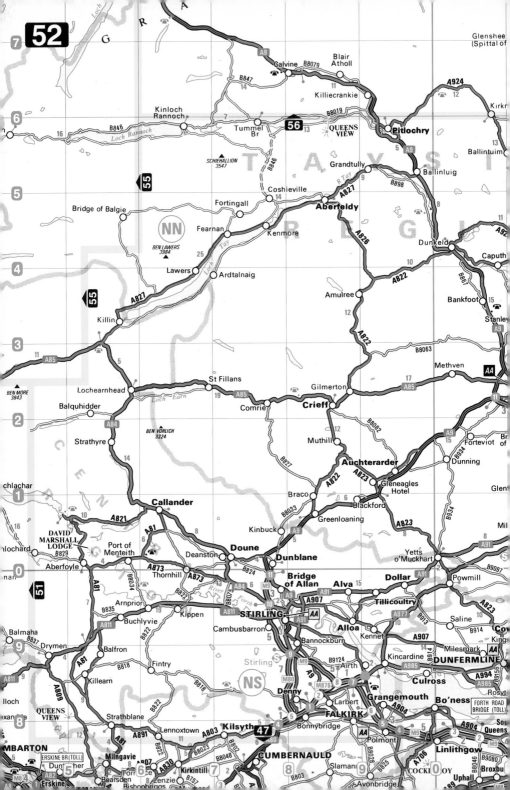

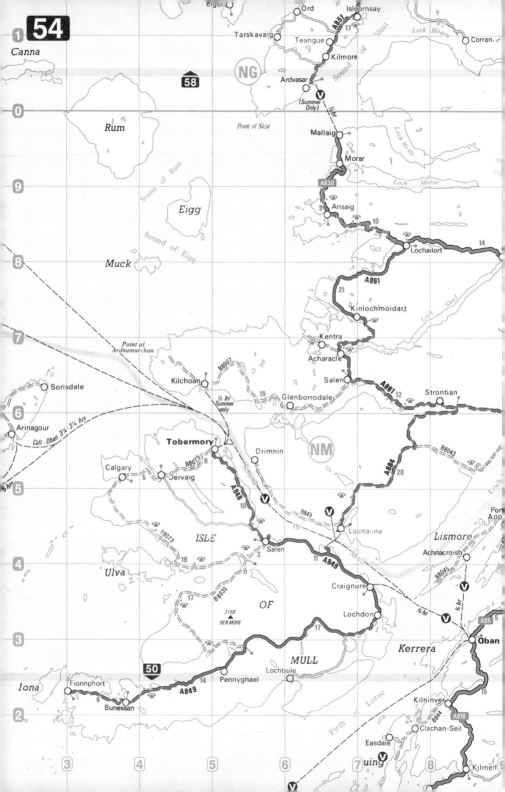

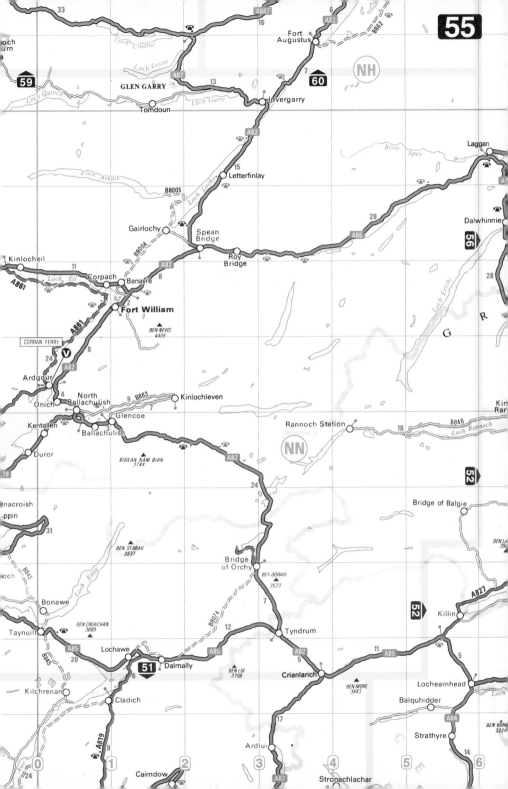

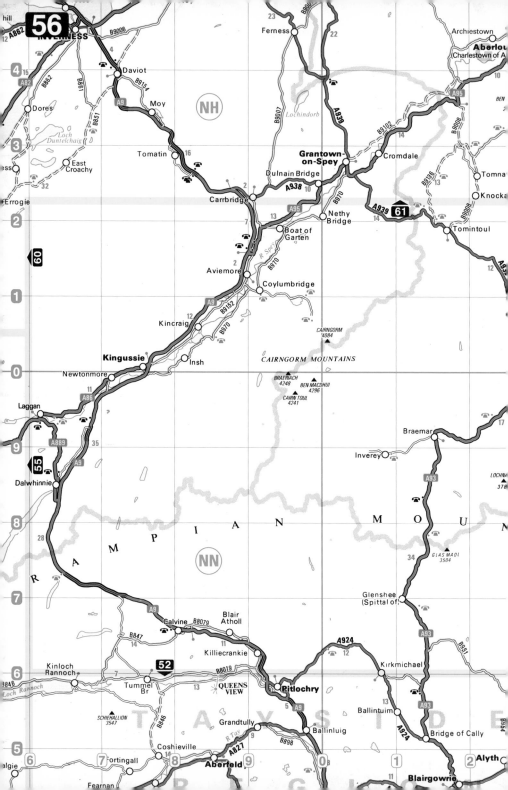

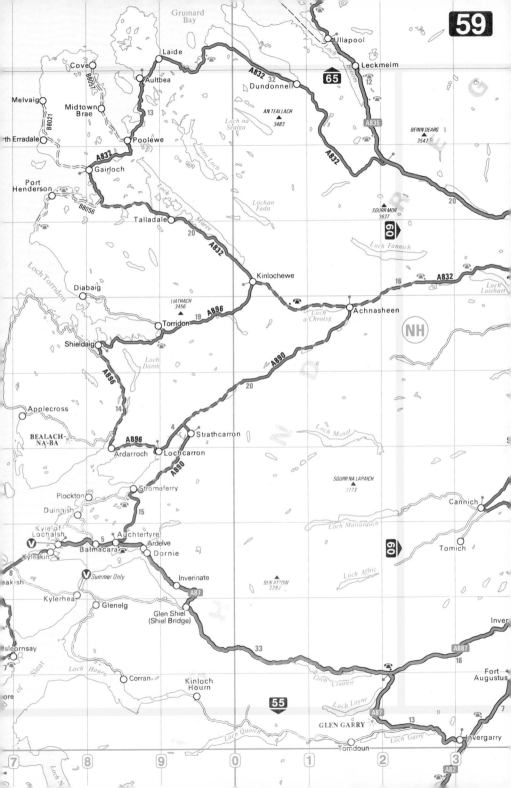

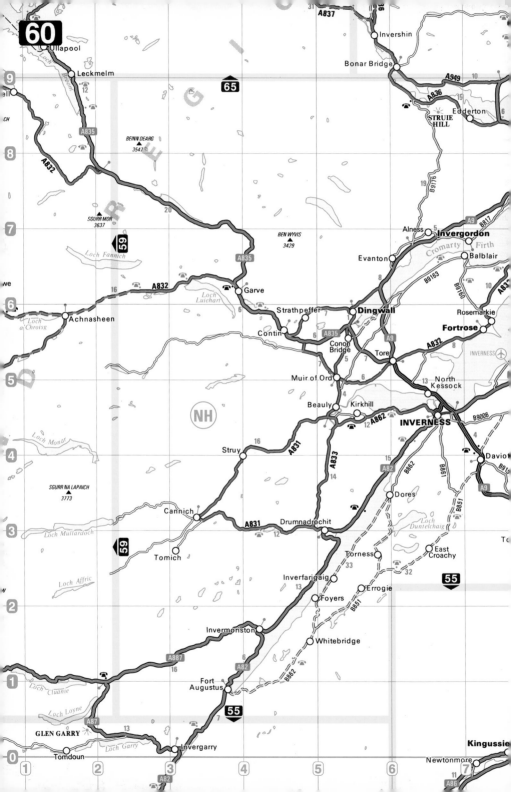

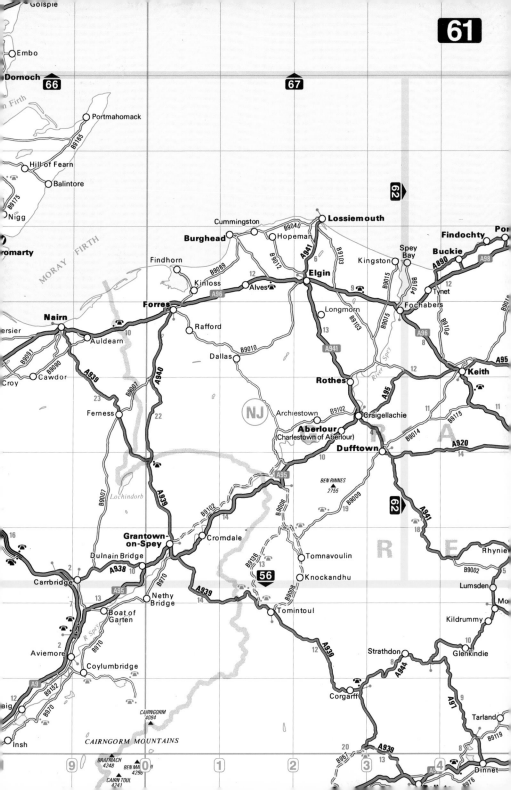

9

67

8

61

Lossiemouth
7

B9103

A941

Findochty **Portknockie**
Cullen

Buckie **Portsoy** Whitehills **Macduff** **Rosehe**

Kingston Spey A890 A98 **Banff** New Aberd
Bay 21 B9031

Elgin 12 A98
9 Tynet 6 8 A97
6 **Longmorn** Fochabers Cornhill 9 B9121 11 A947 15 New New
B9015 B9018 B9022 B105 Byth Pitsligo
13 B9103 A96 A95 B9023 B9025 New
A941 8 B106 20 **Aberchirder** Byth **Cuminestown** 4
othes 12 A95 **Keith** A95 B9170
5 River Spey 11 NJ B9117 **Turriff** 13 B9170 **New Deer**
B9102 Craigellachie B115 11 A97 B9024 Auchterless B992 14 **Methlic**
Aberlour A95 4 B9014 B9022 12 B9001 **Fyvie** B9170
(town of Aberlour) A920 14 **Huntly** B992 17 A947 **Tarves**
4 **Dufftown** A96 23 21 A920 **Oldmeldrum** **Pitme**
BEN RINNES **61** 5 **57** 20 **Pitcaple** 5
2755 Kennethmont A97 Insch Old Rayne **Inverurie** B993 18 A947
19 A941 Rhynie B9002 B992 **Kemnay** B994 **Kintore** B979
3 18 5 **Pitcaple** ABERDEEN A96
Tomnavoulin B9002 **Lumsden** **Mossat** **Alford** **Monymusk** B993 A96 16 Ab
Knockandhu 10 A944 6 8 A980 A944 B9117 27 **Westhill** **Bucksburn**
2 **Kildrummy** Glenkindie A980 B993 Echt B9119 B979
tou 12 A939 **Strathdon** A944 8 A97 9 B9119 25 B9119 **Garlogie** A944
A944 **Lumphanan** 14 **Torphins** B9125 **Peterculter**
Corgarff **Tarland** **Kincardine** A980 A9
1 O'Neil **7** 18 **8**
20 A939 **3** 13 **4** 8 **5** **Aboyne** 24 **6** Potarch A93 B9077
0 B9867 B976 **Dinnet** A93
Ballater **Banchory**

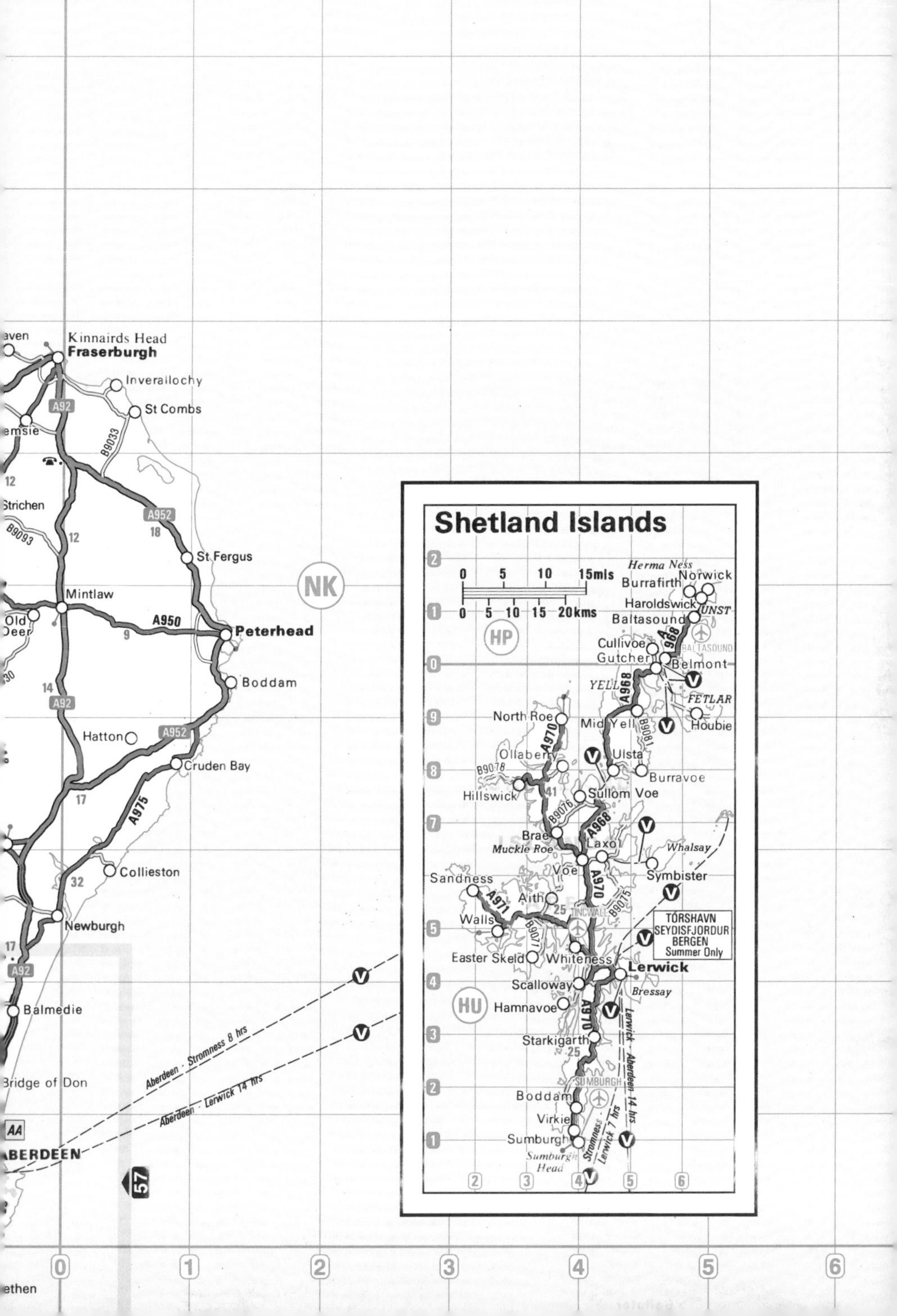

Kinnairds Head
Fraserburgh
aven
Inverailochy
St Combs
emsie
A92
B9033
12
Strichen
A952
18
B9093
12
Old Deer
Mintlaw
A950
9
Peterhead
Boddam
14
A92
Hatton
A952
Cruden Bay
A975
17
Colliestone
32
Newburgh
17
A92
Balmedie
Bridge of Don
AA
ABERDEEN
57
Aberdeen - Stromness 8 hrs
Aberdeen - Lerwick 14 hrs

Shetland Islands

Herma Ness   Norwick
Burrafirth
Haroldswick
Baltasound
UNST
HP
Cullivoe
Gutcher
Belmont
A968
YELL
FETLAR
North Roe
Mid Yell
Houbie
Ollaberry
Ulsta
Burravoe
Hillswick
Sullom Voe
A970
Brae
Laxo
Whalsay
Muckle Roe
Voe
A968
Sandness
Aith
Symbister
Walls
A971
TÓRSHAVN
SEYDISFJORDUR
BERGEN
Summer Only
Easter Skeld
Whiteness
Lerwick
Scalloway
Bressay
HU
Hamnavoe
Starkigarth
25
SUMBURGH
Boddam
Virkie
Sumburgh
Sumburgh Head

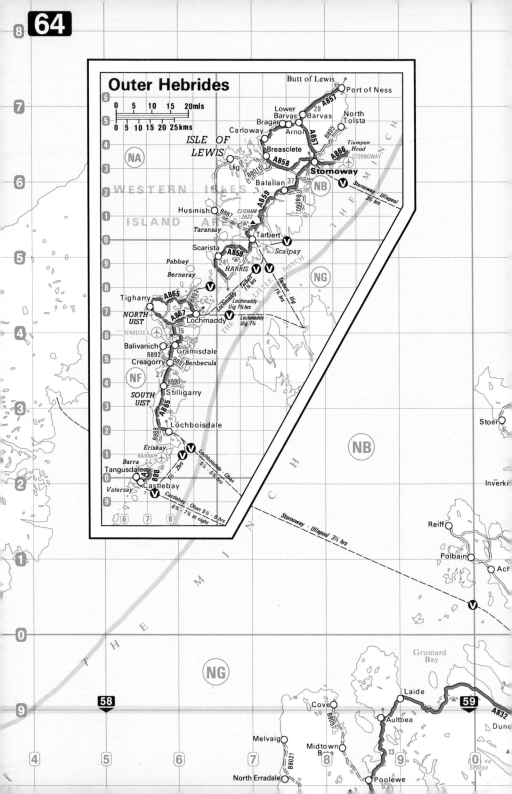

Outer Hebrides

0 5 10 15 20mls

0 5 10 15 20 25kms

ISLE OF LEWIS

NA

WESTERN   ISLES

ISLAND AREA

Butt of Lewis
Port of Ness
Lower Barvas
Barvas
28 A857
North Tolsta
Bragar
Carloway
Arnol
A857
B895
Breasclete
A858
Tiumpan Head
STORNOWAY
A866
Stornoway
Uig
(B801)
Balallan
37
NB
V
Stornoway : Ullapool 3½ hrs
Husinish
B887
CLISHAM 2622
A859
(B8060)
Taransay
Tarbert
Scarista
A859
Scalpay
Pabbay
24
HARRIS
V
Berneray
B893
V
Lochmaddy : Uig 1¾ hrs
THE LITTLE MINCH
Tarbert : Uig 1¾ hrs
NG
Tighharry
A865
NORTH UIST
A867
Lochmaddy
V
Lochmaddy : Uig 1¾
BENBECULA
15
Balivanich
B892
Gramisdale
Creagorry
B892
Benbecula
NF
27
B890
Stilligarry
SOUTH UIST
A865
B888
Lochboisdale
Eriskay
BARRAY
V
V
Lochboisdale : Oban 5½ - 5½ hrs
Barra
½ 2hrs
Tangusdale
B888
Vatersay
Castlebay
V
Castlebay : Oban 5½ - 6 hrs
6¼ 7½ at night
6   7   8

NB

Stornoway : Ullapool 3½ hrs

Stoer

Inverki

Reiff
Polbain
Ach

V

T H E   M I N C H

NG

Gruinard Bay

58
Laide
59
A832
Cove
B8005
Aultbea
Dune
Melvaig
Midtown
B021
na Sealga
North Erradale
Poolewe

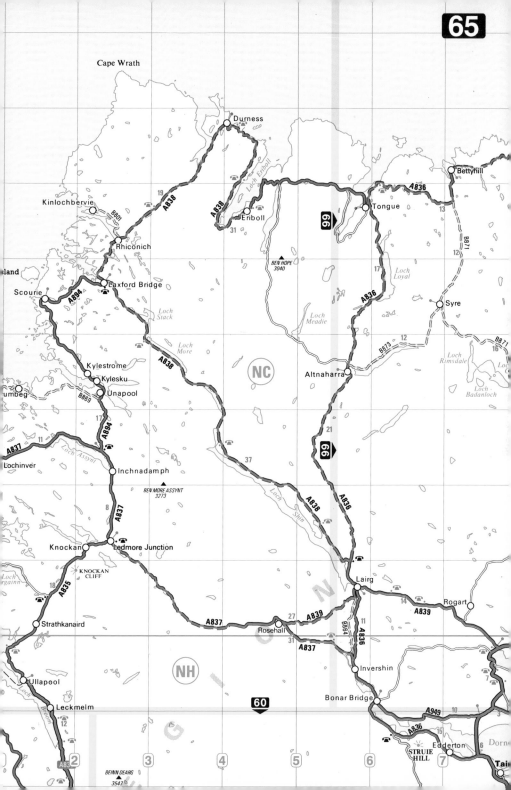

Cape Wrath

Durness

Bettyhill

Kinlochbervie

19 *A838*

B801

A838

A838

Eriboll

Tongue

99

A836

13

B871

31

Rhiconich

12

BEN HOPE
3040

17

Loch
Loyal

Scourie

Laxford Bridge

A894

Loch
Stack

Loch
More

A838

Loch
Meadie

Syre

Loch
Rimsdale

B873

12

B871

16

sland

Kylestrome

Kylesku

Unapool

B869

17

NC

Altnaharra

umbeg

A894

Loch Assynt

A837

11

Lochinver

Inchnadamph

21

99

BEN MORE ASSYNT
3273

Loch
Badanloch

Loch

8

A837

A838

A836

37

Shin

Knockan

Ledmore Junction

KNOCKAN
CLIFF

Lairg

Loch
grainn

18

A835

14

Rogart

A839

Strathkanaird

A837

27 *A839*

Rosehall

11

B864

A836

NH

31

A837

Ullapool

Invershin

7

Leckmelm

60

Bonar Bridge

A949

10

12

A836

15

*A83*2 **2**

3

4

5

6

STRUIE
HILL

Edderton

6

Dorn

7

BEINN DEARG
3547

Tai

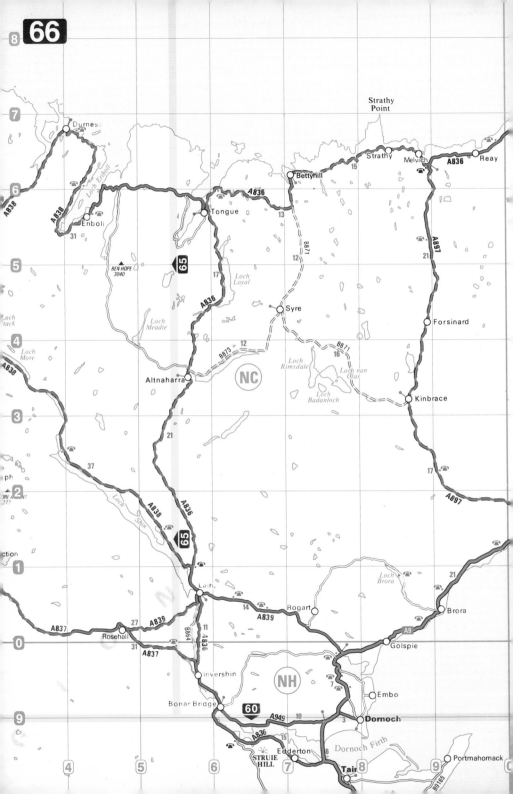

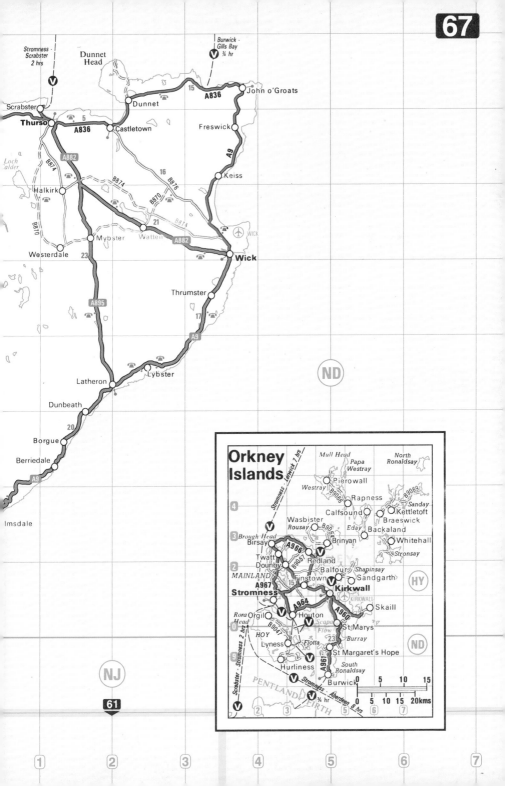

Map symbols

Atlas scale 1:1,000,000 16 miles to 1 inch

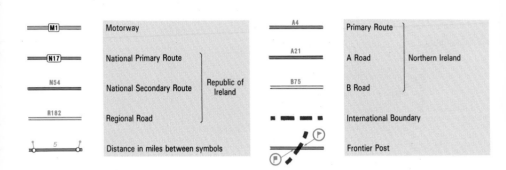

Map pages

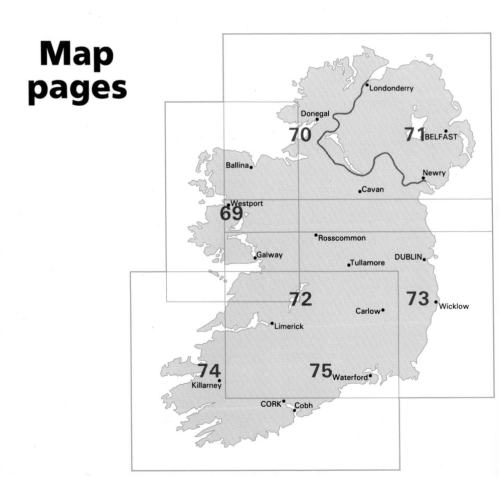

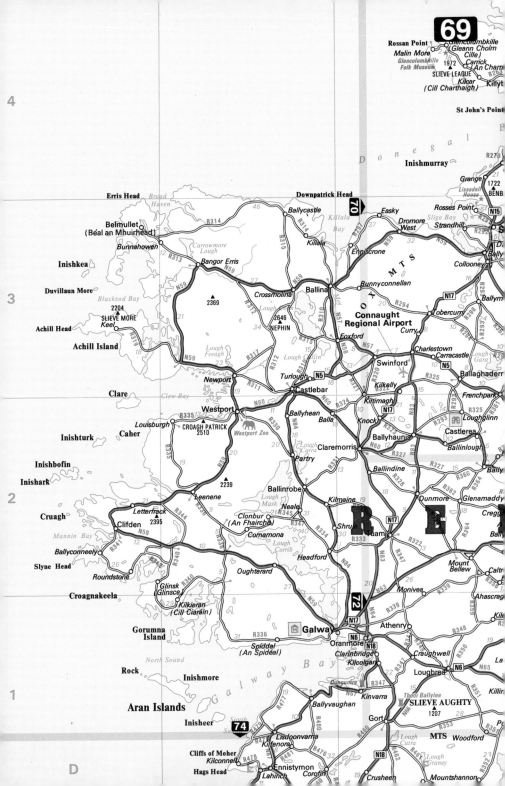

Tory Island
Fanad Head
Horn Head
Bloody Foreland
Dunfanaghy
Rosapenna
R246
R247
Gola
Island
R257
N56
Doe Castle
Cresslough
Rathme
28
Milford
R258
R251
Ray
R259
▲2466
ERRIGAL
Kilmacrenan
Rathm
Aran Island
Crolly
(Croithli)
R254
R245
Dungloe
Letterkenny
R252
R250
N14
Gweebarra Bay
R250
R253
R252
N56
R236
R261
Glenties
Stranorlar
Liffo
Ardara
▲2219
R262
Ballybofey
Clady
Rossan Point
Glencolumbkille
(Gleann Cholm
Cille)
N15
Malin More
1972 ▲
Carrick
(An Charraig)
Lough
Eske
Castlederg
Glencolumbkille
Folk Museum
SLIEVE LEAGUE
Mount
Charles
Kilcar
(Cill Charthaigh)
Killybegs
Dunkineely
Donegal
Drumqu
Donegal
Castle
R232
Ballintra
Lough
Derg
St John's Point
N15
Pettigo
Bay
Ballyshannon
Kesh
White Island Churc
Bundoran
Belleek
Lower Lough
Erne
Inishmurray
R279
Kinlough
Rosscor
Irvinestown
Tully
Castle
B123
Cliffony
Lough
Melvin
Garrison
Derrygonnelly
Grange
Scribbagh
Monea Castle
Balline
Lissadell
House
1722
BENBULBEN
Downpatrick Head
Ballycastle
Killala
Bay
Easky
Dromore
West
Rosses Point
Strandhill
Sligo Bay
N15
Manorhamilton
Belcoo
Enniskillen
Devenish Is.
Castle
Killala
Enniscrone
Sligo
Lough Gill
N16
Glenfarne
Blacklion
Upper
Lough
Erne
Lisbellaw
Dem
Dromahair
Florence
Court
NT
Ca
Crossmolina
Ballina
Bunnyconnellan
Ballysadare
Collooney
R290
R284
Drumkeeran
Dowra
Swanlinbar
IRON
MTS
Nephin
Ballymote
R294
Tobercurry
N17
R299
Ballyfarnan
Keadue
Drumshanbo
Ballinamore
Belturb
Foxford
N57
Curry
Charlestown
Carracastle
N5
Boyle
Leitrim
Fenagh
Killashandra
Swinford
Grallagh
Carrick-
on-Shannon
Carrigallen
Kilkelly
R325
Ballaghaderreen
Drumsna
Mohill
Kiltimagh
N17
Frenchpark
Drumod
Farnaght
Arvagh
Knock
Loughglinn
Elphin
Roosky
Drumlish
Castlebar
Ballyhaunis
Castlerea
Tulsk
Strokestown
Newtown
Forbes
Ballinalee
Granard
Claremorris
Ballinlough
Castleplunkett
Scramoge
Longford
Partry
Ballintober
Cloondara
Killashee
Ballymoe
Lanesborough
Killoe
Edgeworth
Ballinrobe
Ballindine
Dunmore
Glenamaddy
Fuerty
Roscommon
Keenagh
Rathowen
Kilmaine
Clonbur
Nealle
Creggs
Knockcroghery

69
72

Connaught
Regional Airport
Westport Zoo

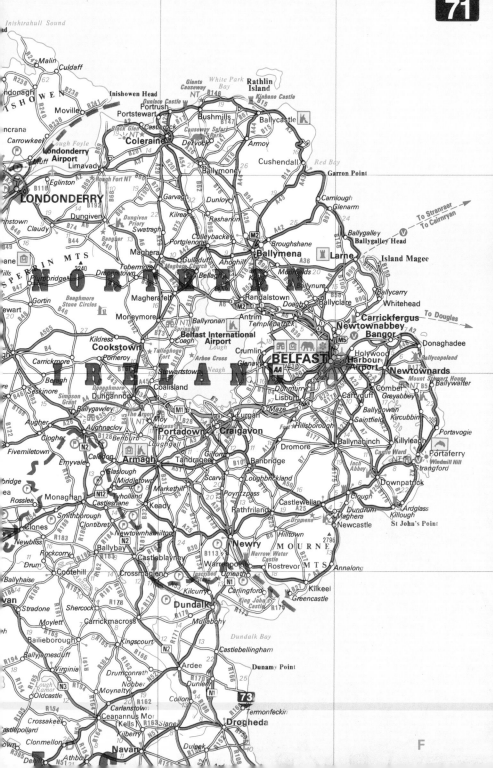

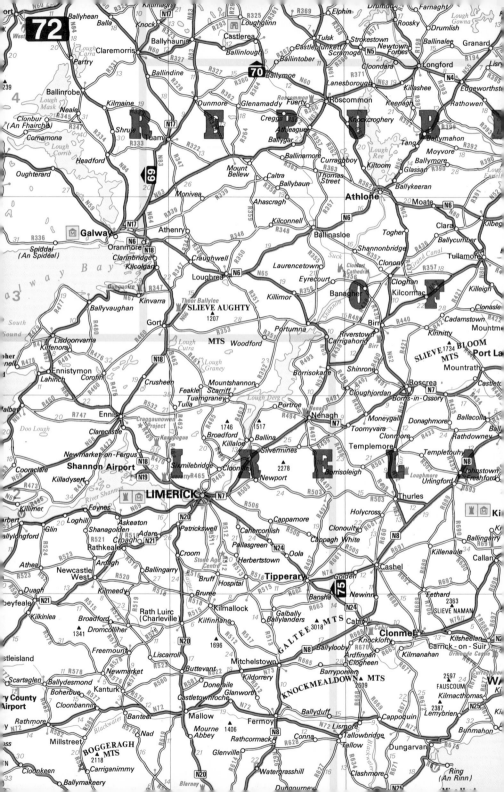

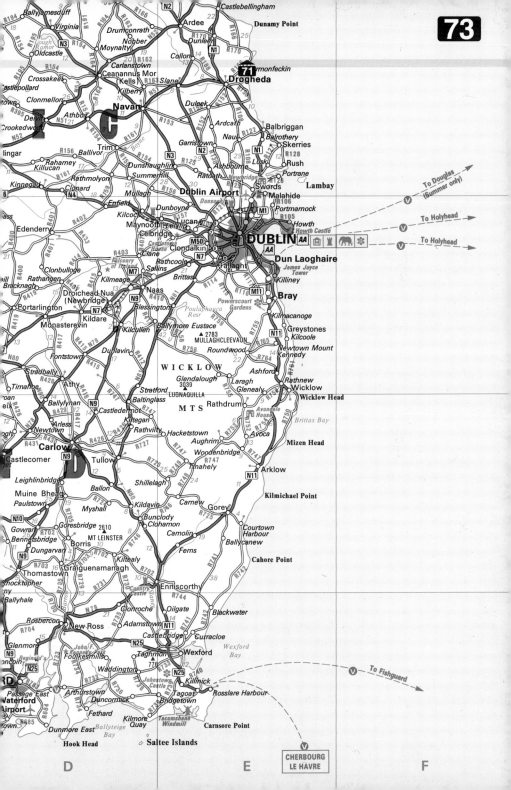

Aran Islands
Inisheer
South Sound

69

Galw

Ballyvaugh

R477 19
R460
R476 32
R479 R481
Lisdoonvarna
Kilfenora
Cliffs of Moher
Kilconnell
Hags Head
Ennistymon
Lahinch
Corofin
R460
R476

Mal Bay
Milltown Malbay
R474
R747
Enni

Mutton
Doo Lough
Clarecastle
N68

Doonbeg
18
Donegal Point
Kilkee
Cooraclare
Newmarket-on-Fer
Shannon Airpo
Killadysert
R487
N67
R473

Killimer
Kilrush
N67
R488
R486
River Shannon
34

Loop Head
Mouth of the Shannon
R551
Tarbert
Foynes
Loghill
17
R551
Glin
Shanagolde
Asl
Ballylongford
R552
R521
Cro
Rathkeale
R553
R524
R523

Ballybunion

Kerry Head
Ballyduff
Listowel
Athea
Ardagh
Newcastle
West
R523
R555
Causeway
R551
20
R523
Duagh
Kilmeedy
R515
Ballyheige
R556
N69
Abbeyfeale
N21
Ballyheige Bay
25
Rough Point
Abbeydorney
19
Kilkinlea
Broadford
Ardfert
R558
Dromcolliher
Brandon Bay
1170
Kilkinlea
1341
Freemount
3127
BRANDON MTN
2713
BEENOSKEE
Tralee
N21
Sybil Point
Camp
2796
N70
Castleisland
Newm
Slea Head
BAURTREGAUM
R559
R578
Dingle
(An Daingean)
Anascaul
R561
Castlemaine
R22
R23
Scartaglen
Ballydesmond
Kantur
R559
Inch
Milltown
R561
Farranfore
Boherbue
R577
Killorglin
R562
Kerry County Airport
Cloonbannin
Glenbeigh
R563
R22
Beaufort
Killarney
Rathmore
N72
Doulus Head
CARRANTUOHILL
3414
Muckross
Millstreet
BOGGERAG MTS
Valentia
Cahirciveen
2539
MULLAGHANATTIN
Killarney National Park
Muckross House
MANGERTON MTN 2756
Cloonkeen
2118
Carriganimr
R565
R566
Molls Gap
33
Ballymakeery
R568
Kilgarvan
N22
Macroo
Kenmare
R569
Waterville
Sneem
N70
Ballingeary (Béal Átha an Ghaorthaidh)
Inchigeelagh
R584
Staigue Fort
Parknasilla
Tahilla
R571
N71
R585
Kilmichael
The Skelligs
Bolus Head
Castle Cove
Caherdaniel
Laragh
2321
KNOCKBOY
Glengarriff
R585
Ballineen
R586
Ennis
Scariff
Ardgroom
R571
R574
2251
Adrigole
N71
Dunmanway
R599
R588
Cod's Head
Allihies
R572
Bantry
R586
Drimoleague
R597
Dursey
Castletownbere
Bear
Durrus
R591
Lean
Clo
Ballydehob
N71
Ross Carbery
R597
R598
Sheep's Head
Toormore
R592
Schull
Skibbereen
R596
Glandore
Mizen Head
Goleen
Castletownshend
Galley H
Crookhaven
Baltimore
Toe Head
Roaringwater Bay
Clear

Dingle Bay
Kenmare R
Bantry Bay
Dunmanus Bay

4

3

2

1

A

B

C

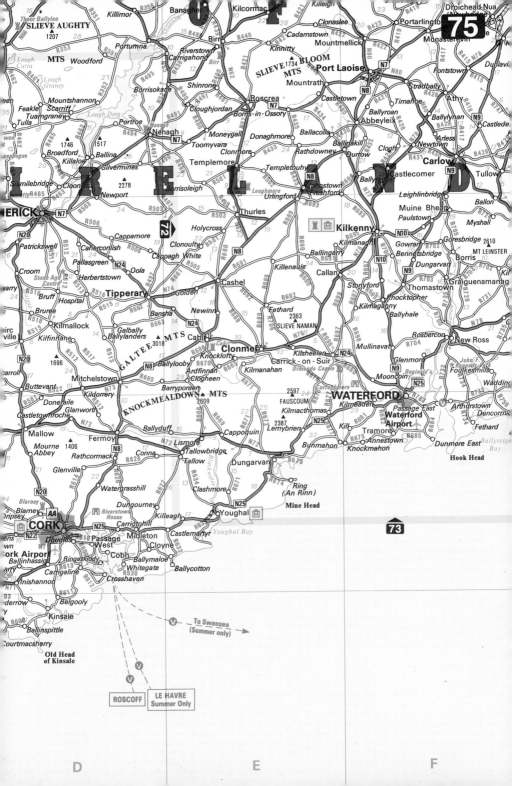

Index to Ireland

Each placename reference in the index gives the page number first, followed by the letter and number of the square in which the particular place can be found.

For example,   Belfast 71 E3 is located on page 71

The letter 'E' refers to the square on the left hand side of the page
The number '3' refers to the square along the bottom of the page.
Belfast can be found within the intersecting square.

Abbeydorney...................... 74 B3	Ballineen............................... 74 C2	Ballysadare.......................... 70 B2
Abbeyfeale 74 C3	Ballingarry........................... 74 C3	Ballyshannon....................... 70 B2
Abbeyleix 72 C2	Ballingarry........................... 72 C2	Ballyvaughan....................... 69 E1
Adamstown........................ 73 D1	Ballingeary (Beal Atha an	Ballywalter........................... 71 F2
Adare................................... 75 D3	Ghaorfthaidh)................... 74 C2	Balrothery............................ 73 E4
Adrigole.............................. 74 B2	Ballinhassig.......................... 75 D2	Baltimore............................. 74 C1
Ahascragh.......................... 72 B3	Ballinlough........................... 70 B1	Baltinglass 73 D2
Ahoghill............................... 71 E3	Ballinrobe............................ 69 E2	Banagher............................. 72 C3
Allihies................................. 74 B1	Ballinspittle......................... 75 D1	Banbridge............................ 71 E2
Anascaul.............................. 74 B2	Ballintober 70 B1	Bandon................................ 75 D2
Annalong............................. 71 E2	Ballintra............................... 70 C3	Bangor 71 F3
Annestown 72 C1	Ballivor................................ 73 D4	Bangor Erris......................... 69 E3
Antrim.................................. 71 E3	Ballon.................................. 73 D2	Bansha................................. 75 E3
Ardagh 74 C3	Ballybaun............................. 72 B4	Banteer................................ 74 C2
Ardara................................. 70 B3	Ballybay 71 D2	Bantry.................................. 74 C1
Ardcath................................ 73 E4	Ballybofey............................ 70 C3	Barryporeen........................ 75 D3
Ardee.................................. 71 E1	Ballybunion 74 B3	Beaufort............................... 74 B2
Ardfert................................. 74 B3	Ballycanew 73 E2	Belcoo.................................. 70 C2
Ardfinnan 72 C1	Ballycarry 71 F3	Belfast.................................. 71 E3
Ardglass.............................. 71 F2	Ballycastle........................... 71 E4	Belgooly............................... 75 D1
Ardgroom............................ 74 B2	Ballycastle........................... 69 E3	Bellaghy 71 E3
Arklow................................. 73 E2	Ballyclare............................. 71 E3	Belleek................................. 70 C2
Arless.................................. 73 D2	Ballyconneely 69 D2	Belmullet (Beal an Mhuirhead) 69 D3
Armagh................................ 71 D2	Ballycotton 75 E2	Belturbet 70 C2
Armoy.................................. 71 E4	Ballycumber 72 C3	Benburb............................... 71 D2
Arthurstown 73 D1	Ballydehob........................... 74 B1	Bennetsbridge...................... 73 D2
Arvagh................................. 70 C1	Ballydesmond...................... 74 C2	Beragh 71 D3
Ashbourne........................... 73 E4	Ballyduff............................... 74 B3	Birr...................................... 72 C3
Ashford................................ 73 E3	Ballyduff............................... 75 E2	Blacklion.............................. 70 C2
Askeaton.............................. 74 C3	Ballyfarnan........................... 70 B2	Blackwater............................ 73 E1
Athboy................................. 73 D4	Balleygalley 71 F3	Blarney................................. 75 D2
Athea................................... 74 C3	Ballygar 72 B4	Blessington 73 E3
Athenry................................ 72 B3	Ballygawley 71 D2	Boherbue.............................. 74 C2
Athleague............................ 72 B4	Ballygowan 71 F2	Borris................................... 73 D2
Athlone 72 C4	Ballyhaise 71 D1	Borris-in-Ossory.................... 72 C3
Athy..................................... 73 D3	Ballyhale............................... 73 D1	Borrisokane.......................... 75 E4
Augher................................. 71 D2	Ballyhaunis 70 B1	Borrisoleigh 72 C2
Aughnacloy.......................... 71 D2	Ballyhean.............................. 69 E2	Boyle.................................... 70 B1
Aughrim 73 E2	Ballyheige 74 B3	Bracknagh 73 D3
Avoca.................................. 73 E2	Ballyjamesduff...................... 71 D1	Bray..................................... 73 E3
	Ballykeeran 72 C4	Bridgetown........................... 73 D1
	Ballylanders 75 D3	Brittas.................................. 73 E3
Bailieborough 71 D1	Ballylongford........................ 74 C3	Broadford............................. 75 D4
Balbriggan........................... 73 E4	Ballylooby 72 C1	Broadford 74 C3
Balla.................................... 69 E2	Ballylynan............................. 73 D2	Broughshane........................ 71 E3
Ballacolla 72 C2	Ballymahon 72 C4	Bruff.................................... 75 D3
Ballaghaderreen 70 B1	Ballymakeery....................... 74 C2	Bruree.................................. 75 D3
Ballina.................................. 69 E3	Ballymaloe 75 E2	Bunclody.............................. 73 D2
Ballina.................................. 75 D4	Ballymena 71 E3	Buncrana 71 D4
Ballinafad............................ 70 B1	Ballymoe 72 B4	Bundoran............................. 70 B2
Ballinagh............................. 70 C1	Ballymoney 71 E4	Bunmahon........................... 72 C1
Ballinakill............................. 73 D2	Ballymore 72 C4	Bunnahowen........................ 69 D3
Ballinalee............................. 70 C1	Ballymore Eustace................ 73 D3	Bunnyconnellan.................... 69 F3
Ballinamallard...................... 70 C2	Ballymote 70 B2	Bushmills.............................. 71 E4
Ballinamore......................... 70 C2	Ballynahinch......................... 71 F2	Butler's Bridge...................... 71 D1
Ballinamore......................... 72 B4	Ballynure 71 E3	Buttevant 75 D3
Ballinascarty 74 C1	Ballyragget........................... 72 C2	
Ballinasloe 72 B3	Ballyroan 73 D3	
Ballindine............................. 72 A4	Ballyronan 71 E3	Cadamstown...................... 72 C3

Caherconlish...... 75 D3
Caherdaniel...... 74 B2
Cahir...... 72 C1
Cahirciveen...... 74 B2
Caledon...... 71 D2
Callan...... 72 C2
Caltra...... 72 B4
Camolin...... 73 E2
Camp...... 74 B3
Cappagh White...... 75 D3
Cappamore...... 75 D3
Cappoquin...... 72 C1
Carlanstown...... 71 D1
Carlingford...... 71 E1
Carlow...... 73 D2
Carndonagh...... 71 D4
Carnew...... 73 E2
Carnlough...... 71 E3
Carracastle...... 70 B1
Carrick (An Charraig)...... 70 B3
Carrickfergus...... 71 F3
Carrickmacross...... 71 D1
Carrickmore...... 71 D3
Carrick-on-Shannon...... 70 C1
Carrick-on-Suir...... 72 C1
Carrigahorig...... 72 B3
Carrigaline...... 75 D2
Carrigallen...... 70 C1
Carriganimmy...... 74 C2
Carrigans...... 71 D3
Carrigtohill...... 75 D2
Carrowkeel...... 71 D4
Carryduff...... 71 F2
Cashel...... 72 C2
Castlebar...... 69 E3
Castlebellingham...... 71 E1
Castleblayney...... 71 D2
Castlebridge...... 73 E1
Castlecomer...... 73 D2
Castle Cove...... 74 B2
Castlederg...... 70 C3
Castledermot...... 73 D2
Castleisland...... 74 C3
Castlemaine...... 74 B2
Castlemartyr...... 75 E2
Castleplunkett...... 70 B1
Castlepollard...... 73 D4
Castlerea...... 70 B1
Castlerock...... 71 D4
Castleshane...... 71 D2
Castletown...... 72 C3
Castletownbere...... 74 B1
Castletownroche...... 75 D2
Castletownshend...... 74 C1
Castlewellan...... 71 E2
Causeway...... 74 B3
Cavan...... 71 D1
Ceanannus Mor (Kells)...... 73 D4
Celbridge...... 73 E3
Charlestown...... 70 B1
Clady...... 70 C3
Clane...... 73 D3
Clara...... 72 C3
Clarecastle...... 74 C4
Claremorris...... 69 F2
Clarinbridge...... 72 A3
Clashmore...... 72 C1
Claudy...... 71 D3
Clifden...... 69 D2
Cliffony...... 70 B2
Clogh...... 73 D2
Cloghan...... 72 C3
Clogheen...... 72 B1
Clogher...... 71 D2
Clohamon...... 73 D2
Clonakilty...... 74 C1

Clonard...... 73 D4
Clonaslee...... 72 C3
Clonbulloge...... 73 D3
Clonbur (An Fhairche)...... 69 E2
Clondalkin...... 73 E3
Clones...... 71 D2
Clonmany...... 71 D4
Clonmel...... 72 C1
Clonmellon...... 73 D4
Clonmore...... 72 C2
Clonony...... 72 C3
Clonoulty...... 72 C2
Clonroche...... 73 D1
Clontibret...... 71 D2
Cloonbannin...... 74 C2
Cloondara...... 70 C1
Cloonkeen...... 74 C2
Cloonlara...... 75 D4
Clough...... 71 F2
Cloughjordan...... 72 C3
Cloyne...... 75 D2
Coagh...... 71 E3
Coalisland...... 71 D2
Cobh...... 75 D2
Coleraine...... 71 E4
Collinstown...... 73 D4
Collon...... 71 E1
Collooney...... 70 B2
Comber...... 71 F2
Conna...... 75 D2
Cookstown...... 71 D3
Coole...... 72 C4
Cooraclare...... 74 C4
Cootehill...... 71 D2
Cork...... 75 D2
Cornamona...... 69 E2
Corofin...... 74 C4
Courtmacsherry...... 75 D1
Courtown Harbour...... 73 E2
Craigavon...... 71 E2
Craughwell...... 72 B3
Creggs...... 72 B4
Cresslough...... 70 C4
Croagh...... 74 C3
Crolly (Croithli)...... 70 B4
Crookedwood...... 73 D4
Crookhaven...... 74 B1
Crookstown...... 74 C2
Croom...... 75 D3
Crossakeel...... 73 D4
Cross Barry...... 75 D2
Crosshaven...... 75 D2
Crossmaglen...... 71 E1
Crossmolina...... 69 E3
Crumlin...... 71 E3
Crusheen...... 74 C4
Culdaff...... 71 D4
Culleybackey...... 71 E3
Curracloe...... 73 E1
Curraghboy...... 72 B4
Curry...... 70 B1
Cushendall...... 71 E4

Daingean...... 73 D3
Delvin...... 73 D4
Derrygonnelly...... 70 C2
Derrylin...... 70 C2
Dervock...... 71 E4
Dingle (An Daingean)...... 74 A2
Doagh...... 71 E3
Donaghadee...... 71 F3
Donaghmore...... 72 C2
Donegal...... 70 C3
Doneraile...... 75 D2
Doonbeg...... 74 C4

Douglas...... 75 D2
Downpatrick...... 71 F2
Dowra...... 70 C2
Draperstown...... 71 D3
Drimoleague...... 74 C1
Dripsey...... 75 D2
Drogheda...... 73 E4
Droichead Nua (Newbridge)... 73 D3
Dromahair...... 70 B2
Dromcolliher...... 74 C3
Dromore...... 71 E2
Dromore...... 70 C2
Dromore West...... 70 B2
Drum...... 71 D2
Drumconrath...... 71 D1
Drumkeeran...... 70 C2
Drumlish...... 70 C1
Drumod...... 70 C1
Drumquin...... 70 C3
Drumshanbo...... 70 C2
Drumsna...... 70 C1
Duagh...... 74 C3
Dublin...... 73 E3
Duleek...... 73 E4
Dunboyne...... 73 E3
Duncormick...... 73 D1
Dundalk...... 71 E1
Dunderrow...... 75 D1
Dundrum...... 71 F2
Dunfanaghy...... 70 C4
Dungannon...... 71 D2
Dungarvan...... 73 D2
Dungarvan...... 72 C1
Dungiven...... 71 D3
Dungloe...... 70 B3
Dungourney...... 75 D2
Dunkineely...... 70 B3
Dun Laoghaire...... 73 E3
Dunlavin...... 73 D3
Dunleer...... 71 E1
Dunloy...... 71 E3
Dunmanway...... 74 C2
Dunmore...... 72 B4
Dunmore East...... 73 D1
Dunmurry...... 71 E2
Dunshauglin...... 73 E4
Durrow...... 72 C2
Durrus...... 74 B1

Easky...... 70 A2
Edenderry...... 73 D3
Edgeworthstown...... 72 C4
Eglinton...... 71 D3
Elphin...... 70 B1
Emyvale...... 71 D2
Enfield...... 73 D3
Ennis...... 74 C4
Enniscorthy...... 73 D2
Enniscrone...... 69 F3
Enniskean...... 74 C2
Enniskillen...... 70 C2
Ennistymon...... 74 C4
Eyrecourt...... 72 B3

Farnaght...... 70 C1
Farranfore...... 74 B2
Feakle...... 75 D4
Fenagh...... 70 C1
Fermoy...... 75 D2
Ferns...... 73 E2
Fethard...... 72 C2
Fethard...... 73 D1
Finnea...... 70 C1
Fintona...... 71 D2

Fivemiletown...... 71 D2
Fontstown...... 73 D3
Foulkesmills...... 73 D1
Foxford...... 69 F3
Foynes...... 74 C3
Freemount...... 74 C3
Frenchpark...... 70 B1
Freshford...... 72 C2
Fuerty...... 72 B4

Galbally...... 75 D3
Galway...... 69 E1
Garrison...... 70 C2
Garristown...... 73 E4
Garvagh...... 71 E3
Geashill...... 73 D3
Gilford...... 71 E2
Glandore...... 74 C1
Glanworth...... 75 D2
Glaslough...... 71 D2
Glassan...... 72 C4
Glenamaddy...... 72 B4
Glenarm...... 71 E3
Glenavy...... 71 E3
Glenbeigh...... 74 B2
Glencolumbkille (Gleann
Cholm Cille)...... 70 B3
Glendalough...... 73 E3
Glenealy...... 73 E3
Glenfarne...... 70 C2
Glengarriff...... 74 B2
Glenmore...... 73 D1
Glenties...... 70 B3
Glenville...... 75 D2
Glin...... 74 C3
Glinsk (Glinsce)...... 69 D2
Golden...... 72 C2
Goleen...... 74 B1
Goresbridge...... 73 D2
Gorey...... 73 E2
Gort...... 72 A3
Gortin...... 71 D3
Gowran...... 73 D2
Graiguenamanagh...... 73 D2
Grallagh...... 70 B1
Granard...... 70 C1
Grange...... 70 B2
Greencastle...... 71 E1
Greyabbey...... 71 F2
Greystones...... 73 E3
Gulladuff...... 71 E3

Hacketstown...... 73 E2
Headford...... 69 E2
Herbertstown...... 75 D3
Hillsborough...... 71 E2
Hilltown...... 71 E2
Hospital...... 75 D3
Holycross...... 72 C2
Holywood...... 71 F3
Howth...... 73 E3

Inch...... 74 B2
Inchigeelagh...... 74 C2
Inishannon...... 75 D2
Irvinestown...... 70 C2

Johnstown...... 72 C2

Kanturk...... 74 C2
Keadue...... 70 C2

Keady...... 71 D2
Keel...... 69 D3
Keenagh...... 72 C4
Kells...... 71 E3
Kenmare...... 74 B2
Kesh...... 70 C2
Kilbeggan...... 72 C3
Kilberry...... 73 D4
Kilbrittain...... 75 D1
Kilcar (Cill Charthaigh)...... 70 B3
Kilcock...... 73 D3
Kilcolgan...... 72 A3
Kilconnell...... 72 B3
Kilconnell...... 74 C4
Kilcoole...... 73 E3
Kilcormac...... 72 C3
Kilcullen...... 73 D3
Kilcurry...... 71 E1
Kildare...... 73 D3
Kildavin...... 73 D2
Kildorrery...... 75 D3
Kildress...... 71 D3
Kilfenora...... 74 C4
Kilfinnane...... 75 D3
Kilgarvan...... 74 C2
Kilkee...... 74 B4
Kilkeel...... 71 E1
Kilkelly...... 70 B1
Kilkenny...... 73 D2
Kilkieran (Cill Ciarain)...... 69 E1
Kilkinlea...... 74 C3
Kill...... 72 C1
Killadysert...... 74 C3
Killala...... 69 E3
Killaloe...... 75 D4
Killarney...... 74 C2
Killashandra...... 70 C1
Killashee...... 72 C4
Killeagh...... 75 E2
Killeigh...... 72 C3
Killenaule...... 72 C2
Killimer...... 74 C3
Killimor...... 72 B3
Killiney...... 73 E3
Killinick...... 73 E1
Killorglin...... 74 B2
Killough...... 71 F2
Killucan...... 73 D4
Killybegs...... 70 B3
Killyleagh...... 71 F2
Kilmaconoge...... 73 E3
Kilmacrenan...... 70 C4
Kilmacthomas...... 72 C1
Kilmaganny...... 72 C2
Kilmaine...... 69 E2
Kilmallock...... 75 D3
Kilmanagh...... 72 C2
Kilmanahan...... 72 C1
Kilmeaden...... 73 D1
Kilmeage...... 73 D3
Kilmeedy...... 74 C3
Kilmichael...... 74 C2
Kilmore Quay...... 73 D1
Kilnaleck...... 71 D1
Kilrea...... 71 E3
Kilrush...... 74 C3
Kilsheelan...... 72 C1
Kiltealy...... 73 D2
Kiltegan...... 73 D2
Kiltimagh...... 70 A1
Kiltoom...... 72 C4
Kingscourt...... 71 D1
Kinlough...... 70 B2
Kinnegad...... 73 D4
Kinnitty...... 72 C3
Kinsale...... 75 D1

Kinvarra...... 69 F1
Kircubbin...... 71 F2
Knock...... 70 A1
Knockcroghery...... 72 C4
Knocklofty...... 72 C1
Knockmahon...... 72 C1
Knocktopher...... 73 D2

Lahinch...... 74 C4
Lanesborough...... 72 C4
Laragh...... 73 E3
Larne...... 71 F3
Lauragh...... 74 B2
Laurencetown...... 72 B3
Leap...... 74 C1
Leenene...... 69 E2
Leighlinbridge...... 73 D2
Leitrim...... 70 C1
Leixlip...... 73 E3
Lemybrien...... 72 C1
Letterfrack...... 69 D2
Letterkenny...... 70 C3
Lifford...... 70 C3
Limavady...... 71 D4
Limerick...... 75 D3
Lisbellaw...... 70 C2
Lisburn...... 71 E2
Liscarroll...... 75 D3
Lisdoonvarna...... 69 E1
Lismore...... 72 C1
Lisnaskea...... 70 C2
Lisryan...... 72 C4
Listowel...... 74 C3
Loghill...... 74 C3
Londonderry...... 71 D3
Longford...... 72 C4
Loughbrickland...... 71 E2
Loughgall...... 71 E2
Loughglinn...... 70 B1
Loughrea...... 72 B3
Louisburgh...... 69 E2
Lucan...... 73 E3
Lurgan...... 71 E2
Lusk...... 73 E4

Macroom...... 74 C2
Maghera...... 71 E3
Maghera...... 71 F2
Magherafelt...... 71 E3
Maguiresbridge...... 70 C2
Malahide...... 73 E4
Malin...... 71 D4
Malin More...... 70 B3
Mallow...... 75 D2
Manorhamilton...... 70 B2
Markethill...... 71 E2
Maynooth...... 73 E3
Maze...... 71 E2
Middletown...... 71 D2
Midleton...... 75 D2
Milford...... 70 C4
Millstreet...... 74 C2
Milltown...... 74 B2
Milltown Malbay...... 74 C4
Mitchelstown...... 75 D3
Moate...... 72 C3
Mohill...... 70 C1
Molls Gap...... 74 B2
Monaghan...... 71 D2
Monasterevin...... 73 D3
Moneygall...... 72 C2
Moneymore...... 71 D3
Monivea...... 72 B3
Mooncoin...... 73 D1

Moorfields 71 E3
Mount Bellew 72 B4
Mount Charles 70 C3
Mountmellick 73 D3
Mountrath 72 C3
Mountshannon 75 D4
Mourne Abbey 75 D2
Moville 71 D4
Moy 71 D2
Moylett 71 D1
Moynalty 71 D1
Moyvore 72 C4
Muckross 74 C2
Muff 71 D4
Muine Bheag 73 D2
Mullabohy 71 E1
Mullagh 73 D4
Mullinavat 73 D1
Mullingar 73 D4
Myshall 73 D2

Naas 73 D3
Nad 74 C2
Naul 73 E4
Navan 73 D4
Neale 69 E2
Nenagh 75 D4
Newbliss 71 D2
Newcastle 71 F2
Newcastle West 74 C3
Newinn 72 C1
Newmarket 74 C3
Newmarket-on-Fergus 74 C4
Newport 69 E3
Newport 75 D4
New Ross 73 D1
Newry 71 E2
Newtown 73 D2
Newtownabbey 71 F3
Newtownards 71 F3
Newtownhamilton 71 E2
Newtownstewart 71 D3
Newtown Butler 71 D2
Newtown Forbes 70 C1
Newtown Mount Kennedy 73 E3
Nobber 71 D1

Oilgate 73 E1
Oldcastle 71 D1
Omagh 71 D3
Omeath 71 E1
Oola 75 D3
Oranmore 72 A3
Oughterard 69 E2
Ovens 75 D2

Pallasgreen 75 D3
Parknasilla 74 B2
Partry 69 E2
Passage East 73 D1
Passage West 75 D2
Patrickswell 75 D3
Paulstown 73 D2
Pettigo 70 C3
Plumbridge 71 D3
Pomeroy 71 D3
Portadown 71 E2
Portaferry 71 F2
Portarlington 73 D3
Portavogie 71 F2
Portglenone 71 E3
Port Laoise 73 D3
Portmarnock 73 E3

Portrane 73 E4
Portroe 75 D4
Portrush 71 E4
Portstewart 71 D4
Portumna 72 B3
Poyntzpass 71 E2

Raharney 73 D4
Randalstown 71 E3
Rasharkin 71 E3
Rathangen 73 D3
Rathcoole 73 E3
Rathcormack 75 D2
Rathdowney 72 C2
Rathdrum 73 E2
Rathfriland 71 E2
Rathkeale 74 C3
Rath Luric (Charleville) 75 D3
Rathmelton 70 C4
Rathmolyon 73 D4
Rathmore 74 C2
Rathmullen 70 C4
Rathnew 73 E3
Rathowen 72 C4
Rathvilty 73 D2
Ratoath 73 E4
Ray 70 C4
Ring (An Rinn) 72 C1
Ringaskiddy 75 D2
Riverstown 72 C3
Rockcorry 71 D2
Roosky 70 C1
Rosapenna 70 C4
Rosbercon 73 D1
Roscommon 72 B4
Roscrea 72 C3
Ross Carberry 74 C1
Rosscor 70 C2
Rosses Point 70 B2
Rosslare Harbour 73 E1
Rosslea 71 D2
Rostrevor 71 E2
Roundstone 69 D2
Roundwood 73 E3
Rush 73 E4

St Johnstown 70 C3
Saintfield 71 F2
Sallins 73 D3
Scarriff 75 D4
Scartaglen 74 C2
Scarva 71 E2
Schull 74 B1
Scramoge 70 C1
Scribbagh 70 C2
Seskinore 71 D2
Shanagolden 74 C3
Shannonbridge 72 C3
Shercock 71 D1
Shillelagh 73 E2
Shinrone 72 C3
Shrule 69 E2
Silvermines 75 D4
Sion Mills 70 C3
Sixmilebridge 75 D4
Skerries 73 E4
Skibbereen 74 C1
Slane 73 E4
Sligo 70 B2
Smithborough 71 D2
Sneem 74 B2
Spiddal (An Spideal) 69 E1
Stewartstown 71 D3
Stonyford 73 D2

Strabane 70 C3
Stradbally 73 D3
Stradone 71 D1
Strandhill 70 B2
Strangford 71 F2
Stranorlar 70 C3
Stratford 73 D3
Strokestown 70 C1
Summerhill 73 D4
Swanlinbar 70 C2
Swatragh 71 E3
Swinford 70 A1
Swords 73 E4

Taghmon 73 D1
Tagoat 73 E1
Tahilla 74 B2
Tallaght 73 E3
Tallow 72 B1
Tallowbridge 72 B1
Tandragee 71 E2
Tang 72 C4
Tarbert 74 C3
Templemore 72 C2
Templepatrick 71 E3
Templetouhy 72 C2
Termonfeckin 73 E4
Thomas Street 72 B4
Thomastown 73 D2
Thurles 72 C2
Timahoe 73 D3
Timoleague 74 C1
Tinahely 73 E2
Tipperary 75 D3
Tobercurry 70 B2
Tobermore 71 D3
Togher 72 C3
Toomyvara 72 C2
Toormoore 74 B1
Tralee 74 B3
Tramore 73 D1
Trim 73 D4
Tuam 72 A4
Tuamgraney 75 D4
Tulla 75 D4
Tullamore 72 C3
Tullow 73 D2
Tulsk 70 B1
Turlough 69 E3
Tyholland 71 D2
Tyrrellspass 72 C3

Urlingford 72 C2

Virginia 71 D1

Waddington 73 D1
Warrenpoint 71 E2
Waterford 73 D1
Watergrasshill 75 D2
Waterville 74 B2
Westport 69 E2
Wexford 73 E1
Whitegate 75 D2
Whitehead 71 F3
Wicklow 73 E3
Woodenbridge 73 E2
Woodford 72 B3

Youghal 75 E2

Index to placenames

Each entry in the index is followed by the atlas page number and then two letters denoting the 100km grid square. The last two figures refer to the west-east and south-north numbered grid lines.

For example   Whitchurch 30 SJ54
Turn to page 30. The major national grid square we are looking at is SJ. The figure '5' is found along the bottom of the page and the second figure '4' is found along the lefthand side of the page. Whitchurch can be found within the intersecting square.

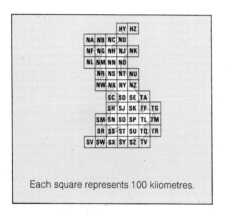

Each square represents 100 kilometres.

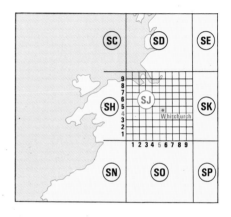

Abberley	23 SO76	Adderbury	24 SP43	Alrewas	31 SK11
Abbey Town	43 NY15	Addington	12 TQ65	Alsager	30 SJ75
Abbots Bromley	31 SK02	Addlestone	17 TQ06	Alston	44 NY74
Abbots Langley	17 TL00	Adlington	34 SD61	Altarnum	5 SX28
Abbotts Salford	24 SP05	Adlington	30 SJ98	Altham	35 SD73
Abbotsbury	9 SY58	Aigburth	30 SJ39	Althorpe	36 SE81
Aberaeron	21 SN46	Ainsdale	34 SD31	Altnaharra	66 NC53
Aberarth	21 SN46	Ainstable	44 NY54	Alton	31 SK04
Aberchirder	62 NJ65	Aintree	34 SJ39	Alton	11 SU73
Abercraf	22 SN81	Airdrie	47 NS76	Altrincham	35 SJ78
Aberdare	14 SO00	Airth	52 NS88	Alva	52 NS89
Aberdaron	28 SH12	Aith	63 HU35	Alvechurch	24 SP07
Aberdeen Airport	57 NJ81	Albrighton	23 SJ80	Alveley	23 SO78
Aberdeen	57 NJ90	Alcester	24 SP05	Alves	61 NJ16
Aberdour	48 NT18	Alconbury	25 TLI7	Alveston	15 ST68
Aberdovey	22 SN69	Aldbrough	37 TA23	Alwalton	25 TL19
Aberfeldy	52 NN84	Aldeburgh	19 TM45	Alwinton	53 NO24
Aberffraw	28 SH36	Alderley Edge	30 SJ87	Alyth	53 NO24
Aberford	36 SE43	Aldermaston	16 SU56	Amberley	15 SO80
Aberfoyle	52 NN50	Alderminster	24 SP24	Amberley	11 TQ01
Abergavenny	23 SO31	Aldershot	11 SU85	Amble	45 NU20
Abergele	29 SH97	Aldridge	24 SK00	Amblecote	23 SO88
Aberlady	48 NT47	Aldwark	40 SE46	Ambleside	39 NY30
Aberlour	61 NJ24	Alexandria	51 NS37	Amersham	17 SU99
Abernethy	53 NO11	Alford	57 NJ51	Amesbury	10 SU14
Aberporth	20 SN25	Alford	33 TF47	Amlwch	28 SH49
Aberriw	29 SJ10	Alfreton	31 SK45	Ammanford	21 SN61
Abersoch	28 SH32	Alfriston	12 TQ50	Ampfield	10 SU32
Abersychan	14 SO20	Allendale	44 NY85	Ampleforth	40 SE57
Abertillery	14 SO20	Allerton	35 SE13	Ampthill	25 TL03
Aberystwyth	22 SN58	Allesley	24 SP28	Ancaster	32 SK94
Abingdon	16 SU49	Allhallows-on-Sea	13 TQ87	Ancroft	49 NU04
Abington	47 NS92	Alloa	52 NS89	Ancrum	48 NT62
Aboyne	57 NO59	Allonby	43 NY04	Andover	10 SU34
Abridge	18 TQ49	Alloway	49 NS31	Andoversford	24 SP01
Accrington	35 SD72	Almondsbury	15 ST68	Andreas	38 SC49
Acharacle	54 NM66	Alness	60 NH66	Angle	20 SM80
Achiltibuie	64 NC00	Alnmouth	45 NV21	Annan	43 NY16
Achnacroish	54 NM84	Alnwick	49 NU11	Annfield Plain	45 NZ15
Achnasheen	59 NH15	Alperton	17 TQ18	Anstey	24 SK50
Acle	27 TG41	Alresford	10 SU53	Anstruther	53 NO50
				Ansty	32 SP38

Appin

Appin	55	NM94
Appleby-in-Westmorland	39	NY62
Applecross	59	NG74
Appledore	6	SS43
Appleton-le-Moors	41	SE78
Arbroath	53	NO64
Archiestown	61	NJ24
Archirondel	9	JS00
Ardarroch	59	NG84
Ardbeg	50	NR44
Ardelve	59	NG82
Arden	51	NS38
Ardentinny	51	NS18
Ardersier	61	NH75
Ardfern	51	NM80
Ardgour	55	NN06
Ardingly	12	TQ32
Ardleigh	19	TM02
Ardlui	51	NN31
Ardlussa	50	NR68
Ardrishaig	51	NR88
Ardrossan	46	NS24
Ardtainaig	52	NN63
Arduaine	51	NM80
Ardvasar	54	NG60
Ardwell	42	NX14
Arinagour	50	NM25
Arisaig	54	NM68
Armadale	47	NS96
Armathwaite	44	NY54
Arncliffe	39	SD97
Arnol	64	NB34
Arnprior	52	NS69
Arnside	39	SD47
Arrochar	51	NN20
Arundel	11	TQ00
Ascog	51	NS16
Ascot	17	SU96
Ash	11	SU85
Ash	13	TR25
Ashbourne	31	SK14
Ashburton	8	SX77
Ashbury	16	SU28
Ashby-de-la-Zouche	31	SK31
Ashby Parva	24	SP58
Ashford	17	TQ07
Ashford	13	TR04
Ashford-in-the-Water	31	SK16
Ashington	45	NZ28
Ashington	11	TQ11
Ashtead	17	TQ15
Ashton Keynes	15	SU09
Ashton-in-Makerfield	34	SJ59
Ashton-under-Lyne	35	SJ99
Askam-in-Furness	38	SD27
Askern	36	SE51
Askrigg	39	SD99
Aspatria	43	NY14
Aspley Guise	25	SP93
Aspull	34	SD60
Aston Clinton	16	SP81
Aston on Clun	23	SO38
Atherstone	24	SP39
Atherton	34	SD60
Attleborough	27	TM09
Auchencairn	43	NX75
Auchterarder	52	NN91
Auchterderran	53	NT29
Auchterhouse	53	NO33
Auchterless	62	NJ74
Auchtermuchty	53	NO21
Achtertyre	59	NG82
Audenshaw	35	SJ99
Audgirth	43	NX98
Audlem	30	SJ64
Aughton	34	SD30
Auldearn	61	NH95
Aultbea	59	NG88
Austwick	39	SD76
Avebury	15	SU17
Aveley	12	TQ57
Aviemore	56	NH81
Avon	10	SZ19
Avonbridge	47	NS97
Avonmouth	14	ST57
Axbridge	14	ST45
Axminster	8	SY29
Aylesbeare	8	SY09
Aylesbury	16	SP81
Aylesford	12	TQ75
Aylsham	27	TG12
Aynho	24	SP53
Ayr	47	NS32
Aysgarth	40	SE08
Ayton	49	NT96
Babbacombe	8	SX96
Backaland	67	HY53
Backwell	14	ST46
Bacton	27	TG33
Bacup	35	SD82
Badmington	15	ST78
Badminton	15	ST88

Bagby	40	SE48
Bagillt	29	SJ27
Baginton	24	SP37
Bagshot	16	SU96
Baguley	35	SJ89
Bagworth	31	SK40
Baillieston	47	NS66
Bainbridge	39	SD98
Bainton	36	SE95
Bakewell	31	SK26
Bala	29	SH93
Balallan	64	NB22
Balbeggie	53	NO12
Balblair	60	NH76
Baldersby	40	SE37
Balderton	32	SK85
Baldock	18	TL23
Baldrine	38	SC48
Balfour	67	HY41
Balfron	52	NS58
Balintore	61	NH87
Balivanich	64	NF75
Ballachulish	55	NN05
Ballantrae	42	NX08
Ballasalla	38	SC27
Ballater	57	NO39
Ballaugh	38	SC39
Ballinluig	52	NN95
Ballintuim	52	NO15
Balloch	51	NS38
Ballygrant	50	NR36
Balmacara	59	NG82
Balmaha	51	NS49
Balmedie	57	NJ91
Balquhidder	52	NN52
Balsall Common	24	SP27
Balsham	18	TL55
Baltasound	63	HP60
Bamburgh	49	NU13
Bamford	31	SK28
Bampton	39	NY51
Bampton	16	SP30
Bampton	7	SS92
Banavie	55	NN17
Banbury	24	SP44
Banchory	57	NO69
Banff	62	NJ66
Bangor	28	SH57
Bangor-on-Dee	30	SJ34
Bankfoot	52	NO03
Banks	34	SD32
Bannockburn	52	NS89
Banstead	12	TQ26
Banwell	18	ST35
Bar Hill	18	TL36
Barbon	39	SD68
Bardney	33	TF16
Bardon Mill	44	NY76
Bardsea	38	SD27
Barford	24	SP26
Barford St Martin	15	SU03
Bargoed	14	ST19
Bargrennan	42	NX37
Barham	13	TR24
Barking	18	TQ48
Barkingside	18	TQ48
Barlby	36	SE63
Barley	18	TL43
Barnby Moor	38	SE74
Barmouth	28	SH61
Barnard Castle	44	NZ01
Barnby Moor	32	SK68
Barnet	18	TQ29
Barnham Broom	27	TG00
Barnoldswick	35	SD84
Barnsley	35	SE30
Barnstaple	6	SS53
Barnton	48	NT17
Barr	42	NX29
Barregarrow	38	SC38
Barrhead	47	NS45
Barrhill	42	NX28
Barrow-in-Furness	38	SD16
Barry Island	7	ST16
Barry	7	ST16
Barton Mills	26	TL77
Barton	34	SD53
Barton Stacey	10	SU44
Barton on Sea	10	SZ29
Barton	18	TL45
Barton under Needwood	31	SK11
Barton upon Humber	37	TA02
Barton-le-Clay	17	TL03
Barvas	64	NB34
Basildon	18	TQ78
Basingstoke	11	SU65
Baslow	31	SK27
Bassenthwaite	44	NY23
Baston	33	TF11
Bath	15	ST76
Bathgate	48	NS96
Batley	35	SE22
Battle	12	TQ71
Baughurst	16	SU56

Birkenhead

Baumber	33	TF27
Bawdeswell	27	TG02
Bawtry	36	SK69
Baycliff	38	SD27
Baydon	16	SU27
Beachley	14	ST59
Beaconsfield	17	SU99
Beadnell	49	NU22
Beaminster	9	ST40
Beare Green	11	TQ14
Bearsden	47	NS57
Beattock	43	NT00
Beaulieu	10	SU30
Beauly	60	NH54
Beaumaris	28	SH67
Beaumont	9	JS00
Bebington	29	SJ38
Beccles	27	TM49
Beckenham	17	TQ36
Beckhampton	15	SU06
Beckington	15	ST85
Becquet Vincent	9	JS00
Bedale	40	SE28
Beddgelert	28	SH54
Beddingham	12	TQ40
Bedford	25	TL04
Bedlington	45	NZ28
Bedlinog	14	SO00
Bedwas	14	ST18
Bedworth	24	SP38
Beeford	37	TA15
Beer	8	SY28
Beeston	30	SJ55
Beeston	32	SK53
Beetham	39	SD47
Beetley	27	TF91
Beith	47	NS35
Belbroughton	24	SO97
Belford	49	NU13
Bellingham	44	NY88
Bellochantuy	46	NR63
Bellshill	47	NS76
Belmont	63	HP50
Belmont	34	SD61
Belper	31	SK34
Belsay	45	NZ07
Belton	36	SE70
Bembridge	11	SZ68
Benderloch	54	NM93
Bentleet	12	TQ78
Benllech Bay	28	SH58
Benson	16	SU69
Bentley	36	SE50
Benwick	26	TL39
Bere Alston	5	SX46
Bere Ferrers	5	SX46
Bere Regis	9	SY89
Berkeley Road	15	SO70
Berkeley	15	ST69
Berkhamsted	17	SP90
Bernisdale	58	NG45
Berriedale	67	ND12
Berrow	14	ST26
Berrynarbor	6	SS54
Berwick	12	TQ50
Berwick-upon-Tweed	49	NT95
Bethersden	13	TQ94
Bethesda	28	SH66
Bettyhill	66	NC70
Betws-Y-Coed	29	SH75
Beulah	22	SN95
Beverley	37	TA03
Bewdley	23	SO77
Bexhill-on-Sea	12	TQ70
Bexley	12	TQ47
Bexleyheath	12	TQ47
Bibury	15	SP10
Bicester	16	SP52
Bickleigh	6	SS90
Biddenden	13	TQ83
Biddulph	30	SJ85
Bideford	6	SS42
Bidford-on-Avon	24	SP15
Bigbury-on-Sea	5	SX64
Biggar	48	NT03
Biggar	38	SD16
Biggin Hill	12	TQ45
Biggleswade	25	TL14
Bilbrook	7	ST04
Bilbrough	36	SE54
Bildeston	19	TL94
Billericay	18	TQ69
Billesley	24	SP15
Billinge	34	SD50
Billingham	40	NZ42
Billingshurst	11	TQ02
Bilston	24	SO99
Binbrook	37	TF29
Bingley	35	SE13
Birchgrove	21	SS79
Birchington	13	TR36
Birdlip	24	SO91
Birdwood	23	SO71
Birkenhead	34	SJ38

Place	Page	Grid
Birmingham Airport	24	SP18
Birmingham NEC	24	SP18
Birmingham	24	SP08
Birsay	67	HY22
Birstall	35	SE22
Bishop Auckland	40	NZ22
Bishop's Castle	23	SO38
Bishop's Frome	23	SO64
Bishop's Lydeard	14	ST12
Bishop's Stortford	18	TL42
Bishop's Tawton	6	SS53
Bishopbriggs	47	NS67
Bishops Waltham	10	SU51
Bishopsteignton	8	SX97
Bishopton	51	NS47
Blaby	24	SP59
Black Torrington	6	SS40
Blackburn	48	NS96
Blackburn	34	SD62
Blackeney	27	TG04
Blackford	52	NN80
Blackmill	21	SS98
Blackpool	34	SD33
Blackrod	34	SD61
Blackwater	10	SZ58
Blackwaterfoot	46	NR92
Blackwell	24	SO97
Blackwood	14	ST19
Blaenau Ffestiniog	28	SH74
Blaenavon	14	SO20
Blaengarw	21	SS99
Blagdon	14	ST45
Blair Atholl	56	NN86
Blairgowrie	53	NO14
Blakeney	15	SO60
Blanchland	45	NY95
Blandford Forum	9	ST80
Blawith	38	SD28
Blaxton	36	SE60
Blaydon	45	NZ16
Bleddfa	22	SO26
Bletchley	25	SP83
Blickling	27	TG12
Blidworth	31	SK55
Blockley	24	SP13
Bloxham	24	SP43
Blubberhouses	40	SE15
Blue Anchor	7	ST04
Blundellsands	38	SD39
Blyth	45	NZ38
Blyth	32	SK68
Blyton	36	SK89
Bo'ness	48	NT08
Boat of Garten	56	NH91
Bodelwyddan	29	SJ07
Boddam	63	HU31
Boddam	63	NK14
Bodfari	29	SJ06
Bodinnick	5	SX15
Bodmin	5	SX06
Bognor Regis	11	SZ99
Boldon	45	NZ36
Bollington	31	SJ97
Bolney	12	TQ22
Bolsover	32	SK47
Bolton Abbey	35	SE05
Bolton Bridge	35	SE05
Bolton	34	SD70
Bolton-le-Sands	39	SD46
Bomere Heath	30	SJ41
Bonar Bridge	66	NH69
Bonawe	55	NN03
Bonchester Bridge	44	NT51
Bonnybridge	52	NS88
Bonnyrigg	48	NT36
Bontddu	28	SH61
Bonvilston	14	ST07
Boot	38	NY10
Bootle	38	SD18
Bootle	34	SJ39
Bordeaux	34	GN00
Bordon	11	SU73
Boreham Street	12	TQ61
Boreham	18	TL70
Borehamwood	17	TQ19
Borgue	67	ND12
Borgue	43	NX64
Borough Green	12	TQ65
Boroughbridge	40	SE36
Borrowdale	38	NY21
Borth	22	SN68
Boscastle	5	SX09
Bosham	11	SU80
Boston	33	TF34
Botcheston	24	SK40
Botesdale	27	TM07
Bothel	43	NY13
Bothwell	47	NS75
Botley	10	SU51
Bottesford Segebrook	32	SK83
Bottisham	18	TL56
Bottom O'th Moor	34	SD71
Boughton Monchelsea	12	TQ75
Boughton	13	TR05
Bouley Bay	9	JS00
Bourne End	16	SU88
Bourne	33	TF02
Bournemouth	10	SZ09
Bourton-on-the-Water	24	SP12
Bovey Tracey	8	SX87
Bovingdon	17	TL00
Bowdon	30	SJ84
Bowes	39	NY91
Bowmore	50	NR35
Bowness-on-Windermere	39	SD49
Box	15	ST86
Bozeat	25	SP95
Bracklesham Bay	11	SZ89
Brackley	25	SP53
Bracknell	16	SU86
Bracknett	16	SU86
Braco	52	NN80
Bradford	35	SE13
Bradford on Avon	15	ST86
Brading	10	SZ68
Bradley Stoke	15	ST68
Bradwell	31	SK18
Bradwell-on-Sea	19	TM00
Bradworthy	6	SS31
Brae	63	HU36
Braemar	56	NO19
Braeswick	67	HY63
Braintree	18	TL72
Braithwaite	38	NY22
Braithwell	36	SK59
Bramber	11	TQ11
Bramhall	30	SJ88
Bramhope	35	SE24
Bramley	36	SK49
Brampton	44	NY56
Brampton	25	TL27
Brancaster Staithe	26	TF74
Brancaster	26	TF74
Brancepeth	45	NZ23
Brandon	25	SP47
Brandon	26	TL78
Brands Hatch	12	TQ56
Branksome	10	SZ09
Bransford	23	SO75
Branston	32	TF06
Branton	36	SE60
Bratton Cloverly	5	SX49
Braunton	6	SS43
Bray	16	SU98
Brayford	6	SS63
Breadsall	31	SK33
Breakish	59	NG62
Bream	15	SO60
Brean	14	ST25
Breasclete	64	NB33
Breaston	31	SK43
Brechfa	21	SN53
Brechin	57	NO56
Brecon	22	SO02
Bredhurst	12	TQ76
Bredon	24	SO93
Bredwardine	23	SO34
Brendon	7	SS74
Brent Knoll	14	ST35
Brentford	17	TQ17
Brentwood	18	TQ59
Brenzett	13	TR02
Bretby	31	SK22
Bretton	35	SE21
Bride	38	NX40
Bridge of Allan	52	NS78
Bridge of Balgie	52	NN54
Bridge of Cally	53	NO15
Bridge of Don	57	NJ90
Bridge of Earn	52	NO11
Bridge of Orchy	55	NN23
Bridge of Weir	51	NS36
Bridgend	50	NR36
Bridgend	21	SS97
Bridgnorth	23	SO79
Bridgwater	14	ST33
Bridlington	41	TA16
Bridport	9	SY49
Brierfield	35	SD83
Brierley Hill	24	SO98
Brigg	37	TA00
Brighouse	35	SE12
Brighstone	10	SZ48
Brighton	12	TQ30
Brimington	32	SK47
Brinklow	24	SP47
Brinyan	67	HY42
Brislington	15	ST67
Bristol Airport	14	ST56
Bristol	15	ST57
Briton Ferry	21	SS79
Brixham	8	SX95
Brixworth	25	SP77
Broad Haven	20	SM81
Broadford	58	NG62
Broadstairs	13	TR36
Broadway	24	SP03
Broadwindsor	9	ST40
Brock	34	SD54
Brockenhurst	10	SU30
Brodick	46	NS03
Bromborough	30	SJ38
Brome	27	TM17
Bromham	25	TL05
Bromley	12	TQ46
Brompton-on-Swale	40	SE29
Bromsgrove	24	SO97
Bromyard	23	SO65
Brook	10	SU21
Brooke	27	TM29
Brookwood	17	SU95
Broomhill	45	NU20
Brora	66	NC90
Brotton	41	NZ61
Brough	39	NY71
Broughton	48	NT13
Broughton	34	SD53
Broughton	10	SU33
Broughton-in-Furness	38	SD28
Broughty Ferry	53	NO43
Brownhills	31	SK00
Broxbourne	17	TL30
Broxburn	48	NT07
Broxted	18	TL52
Broxton	30	SJ45
Bruichladdich	50	NR26
Bruton	15	ST63
Bryn	34	SD50
Brynamman	21	SN71
Bryneglwys	29	SJ14
Brynmawr	14	SO11
Bubwith	36	SE73
Buchhaven	53	NT39
Buchlyvie	52	NS59
Buckden	39	SD97
Buckden	25	TL16
Buckhaven	53	NT39
Buckhurst Hill	18	TQ49
Buckie	62	NJ46
Buckingham	25	SP63
Buckland Newton	9	ST60
Buckland	24	SP03
Bucklers Hard	10	SU40
Buckley	29	SJ26
Bucklfastleigh	8	SX76
Bucklow Hill	30	SJ78
Bucknall	30	SJ84
Bude	6	SS20
Budleigh Salterton	8	SY08
Bugbrooke	25	SP65
Builth Wells	22	SO05
Bulkington	24	SP38
Bulphan	18	TQ68
Bunessan	54	NM32
Bungay	27	TM38
Buntingford	17	TL32
Bunwell	27	TM19
Burbage	15	SU26
Bures	19	TL93
Burford	16	SP21
Burgess Hill	12	TQ31
Burgh Heath	12	TQ25
Burgh-by-Sands	44	NY35
Burghead	61	NJ16
Burlescombe	7	ST01
Burley in Wharfdale	35	SE14
Burley	10	SU20
Burleydam	30	SJ64
Buriton	30	SJ42
Burneston	40	SE38
Burnham Deepdale	26	TF84
Burnham Market	26	TF84
Burnham	17	SU98
Burnham-on-Crouch	19	TQ99
Burnham-on-Sea	14	ST34
Burnley	35	SD83
Burnopfield	45	NZ15
Burnsall	40	SE06
Burnt Yates	40	SE26
Burntisland	48	NT28
Burntwood	31	SK00
Burrafirth	63	HP61
Burravoe	63	HU57
Burrelton	52	NO13
Burrington	6	SS61
Burry Port	21	SN40
Burscough Bridge	34	SD41
Burscough	34	SD41
Burslem	30	SJ84
Burton Agnes	41	TA16
Burton Bradstock	9	SY48
Burton Latimer	25	SP97
Burton upon Trent	31	SK22
Burton-on-Stather	36	SE81
Burwash	12	TQ62
Burwell	18	TL56
Burwick	67	ND48
Bury	35	SD81
Bury St Edmunds	19	TL86
Bury	11	TQ09
Bushy	47	NS55
Bushey	17	TQ19

Butley

Butley ... 19 TM35
Buttermere ... 38 NY11
Buxton ... 31 SK07
Bwlch ... 22 SO12
Byfleet ... 17 TQ06
Bylchau ... 29 SH96

Cadnam ... 10 SU31
Caeathro ... 28 SH56
Caergwrle ... 29 SJ35
Caerleon ... 14 ST39
Caernarfon ... 28 SH46
Caerphilly ... 14 ST18
Caersws ... 22 SO09
Caerwent ... 14 ST49
Cairndow ... 51 NN11
Cairnryan ... 42 NX06
Caister-on-Sea ... 27 TG51
Caistor ... 37 TA10
Calbourne ... 10 SZ48
Caldbeck ... 44 NY34
Calder Bridge ... 38 NY00
Caiderbrook ... 35 SD91
Caldercruix ... 47 NS86
Caldich ... 51 NN02
Calfsound ... 67 HY53
Calgary ... 54 NM35
Callander ... 52 NN60
Callington ... 5 SX36
Calne ... 15 ST97
Calvine ... 13 TQ91
Camber ... 56 NN86
Camberley ... 16 SU86
Camborne ... 4 SW64
Cambridge ... 15 SO70
Cambridge ... 18 TL45
Cambusbarron ... 52 NS79
Cambuslang ... 47 NS66
Camelford ... 4 SX08
Campbeltown ... 46 NR72
Campsea Ash ... 19 TM35
Candlesby ... 33 TF46
Canford Cliffs ... 10 SZ08
Cannich ... 60 NH33
Cannock ... 31 SJ91
Canonbie ... 44 NY47
Canterbury ... 13 TR15
Canvey Island ... 18 TQ78
Caoles ... 50 NMO4
Capel Curig ... 28 SH75
Capel Hendre ... 21 SN51
Capel ... 11 TQ14
Caputh ... 52 NO04
Carbis Bay ... 4 SW53
Carbost ... 58 NG33
Cardiff ... 14 ST17
Cardigan ... 20 SN14
Cardross ... 51 NS37
Carfraemill ... 48 NT55
Carisbrooke ... 10 SZ48
Cark ... 39 SD37
Carlisle ... 44 NY45
Carlops ... 48 NT15
Carloway ... 64 NB34
Carlton ... 40 SE08
Carluke ... 47 NS85
Carlyon Bay ... 5 SX05
Carmarthen ... 21 SN42
Carnforth ... 39 SD47
Carhoustie ... 53 NO53
Carnwath ... 48 NS94
Carperby ... 40 SE08
Carradale ... 46 NR83
Carrbridge ... 61 NH92
Carrefour Selous ... 9 JS00
Carrutherstown ... 43 NY17
Carrville ... 45 NZ34
Carsphairn ... 42 NX59
Carstairs ... 47 NS94
Carter Bar ... 44 NT60
Carterton ... 16 SP20
Cartmel ... 39 SD37
Castel ... 38 GN00
Casterton ... 39 SD67
Castle Ashby ... 25 SP85
Castle Bromwich ... 24 SP18
Castle Cary ... 15 ST63
Castle Combe ... 15 ST87
Castle Donington ... 31 SK42
Castle Douglas ... 43 NX76
Castle Rising ... 26 TF62
Castlebay ... 64 NL69
Castleford ... 36 SE42
Castlemartin ... 20 SR99
Castleside ... 45 NZ04
Castleton ... 41 NZ60
Castleton ... 31 SK18
Castleton ... 14 ST28
Castletown ... 38 SC26
Castletown ... 67 ND16
Castletown ... 38 SC26
Caterham ... 12 TQ35
Caton ... 39 SD56

Catterick Bridge ... 40 SE29
Catterick Garrison ... 40 SE19
Cautley ... 39 SD69
Cavendish ... 18 TL84
Caversham ... 16 SU77
Cawdor ... 61 NH85
Cawood ... 36 SE53
Cawston ... 27 TG12
Caxton ... 18 TL35
Cemaes Bay ... 28 SH39
Cemmaes Road ... 22 SH80
Cerne Abbas ... 9 ST60
Cerrigydrudion ... 29 SH94
Chacewater ... 4 SW74
Chaddesley Corbett ... 23 SO87
Chadlington ... 16 SP32
Chadwell Heath ... 12 TQ48
Chagford ... 8 SX78
Chale ... 10 SZ47
Chale ... 10 SZ47
Chalfont St Peter ... 17 TQ09
Chalford ... 15 SO80
Chalgrove ... 16 SU69
Challock ... 13 TRO5
Chandler's Ford ... 10 SU42
Chapel St Leonards ... 33 TF57
Chapel-en-le-Frith ... 31 SK08
Chapelton ... 47 NS64
Chapeltown ... 36 SK39
Chard ... 8 ST30
Chardstock ... 8 ST30
Charfield ... 15 ST79
Charing ... 13 TQ94
Charingworth ... 24 SP13
Charlbury ... 16 SP31
Charlecote ... 24 SP25
Charlesworth ... 35 SK09
Charlton Marshall ... 9 ST80
Charlwood ... 11 TQ24
Charmouth ... 9 SY39
Charnock Richard ... 34 SD51
Chatburn ... 35 SD74
Chatham ... 12 TQ76
Chattenden ... 12 TQ77
Chatteris ... 26 TL38
Chatton ... 49 NU02
Chawleigh ... 6 SS71
Cheadle Hulme ... 30 SJ88
Cheadle ... 35 SJ88
Cheadle ... 31 SK04
Cheam ... 12 TQ26
Cheddar ... 14 ST45
Chelford ... 30 SJ87
Chelmsford ... 18 TL70
Chelsfield ... 12 TQ46
Cheltenham ... 24 SO92
Chelwood Gate ... 12 TQ43
Chelwood ... 15 ST66
Chenies ... 17 TQ09
Chepstow ... 14 ST59
Cheriton Bishop ... 8 SX79
Cheriton Fitzpaine ... 7 SS80
Chertsey ... 17 TQ06
Chesham ... 17 SP90
Cheshunt ... 17 TL30
Chessington ... 17 TQ16
Chester ... 30 SJ46
Chester-le-Street ... 45 NZ25
Chesterfield ... 31 SK37
Chesterton ... 30 SJ84
Chichester ... 11 SU80
Chiddingfold ... 11 SU93
Chigwell ... 18 TQ49
Chilcompton ... 15 ST65
Chilham ... 13 TRO5
Chillington ... 8 SX74
Chilmark ... 15 ST93
Chilwell ... 32 SK53
Chingford ... 18 TQ39
Chinnor ... 16 SP70
Chippenham ... 15 ST97
Chipperfield ... 17 TL00
Chipping ... 34 SD64
Chipping Campden ... 24 SP13
Chipping Norton ... 24 SP32
Chipping ... 34 SD64
Chirbury ... 23 SO29
Chirk ... 29 SJ23
Chirnside ... 49 NT85
Chiseldon ... 15 SU17
Chiselhurst ... 12 TQ47
Chittlehamholt ... 6 SS62
Chobham ... 17 SU96
Chollerford ... 45 NY97
Chorley ... 34 SD51
Chorleywood ... 17 TQ09
Chorlton ... 30 SJ44
Christchurch ... 23 SO51
Christchurch ... 10 SZ19
Chudleigh Knighton ... 8 SX87
Chudleigh ... 8 SX87
Chulmleigh ... 6 SS61
Church Stoke ... 23 SO29
Church Stretton ... 23 SO49

Corby

Churston Ferrers ... 8 SX95
Churt ... 11 SU83
Cilgerran ... 20 SN14
Cinderford ... 23 SO61
Cirencester ... 15 SP00
Clachan ... 46 NR75
Clachan-Seil ... 51 NM71
Clacton-on-Sea ... 19 TM11
Cladich ... 51 NN02
Clanfield ... 16 SP20
Claonaig ... 46 NR85
Clapham ... 39 SD76
Clapham ... 25 TL06
Clarach ... 22 SM68
Clare ... 18 TL74
Clarencefield ... 43 NY06
Clavering ... 18 TL43
Clawton ... 6 SX39
Clayton-le-Moors ... 35 SD73
Clearwell ... 14 SO50
Cleator Moor ... 38 NY01
Cleckheaton ... 35 SE12
Cleethorpes ... 37 TA30
Cleeve Hill ... 24 SO92
Cleeve ... 14 ST46
Cleland ... 47 NS75
Cleobury Mortimer ... 23 SO67
Cleobury North ... 23 SO68
Clevedon ... 14 ST47
Cleveleys ... 34 SD34
Cley next the Sea ... 27 TG04
Cliffe ... 12 TQ77
Clifton ... 34 SD43
Cliftonville ... 13 TR37
Climping ... 11 TQ00
Clitheroe ... 35 SD74
Clophill ... 25 TL03
Cloughton ... 41 TA09
Clova ... 57 NO37
Clovelly ... 6 SS32
Clowne ... 32 SK47
Clun ... 23 SO28
Clydebank ... 47 NS47
Clynder ... 51 NS28
Clynnogfawr ... 28 SH44
Clyro ... 22 SO24
Clyst Honiton ... 8 SX99
Coalville ... 31 SK41
Coatbridge ... 47 NS76
Cobham ... 17 TQ16
Cobridge ... 30 SJ84
Cockburnspath ... 49 NT77
Cockenzie ... 48 NT47
Cockermouth ... 43 NY13
Coddenham ... 19 TM15
Codicote ... 17 TL21
Codnor ... 31 SK44
Codsall ... 23 SJ80
Coggeshall ... 19 TL82
Colby ... 38 SC27
Colchester ... 19 TL92
Coldingham ... 49 NT96
Coleford ... 15 SO51
Colerne ... 15 ST87
Coleshill ... 24 SP28
Colinton ... 48 NT26
Colintraive ... 51 NS07
Collieston ... 63 NK12
Collin ... 43 NY07
Collingham ... 36 SE34
Collington ... 23 SO66
Colnbrook ... 17 TQ07
Colne ... 35 SD84
Coln St Aldwyns ... 15 SP10
Colsterworth ... 33 SK92
Coltishall ... 27 TG21
Colvend ... 43 NX85
Colwich ... 31 SK02
Colwyn Bay ... 29 SH87
Colyton ... 8 SY29
Combe Martin ... 6 SS84
Combeinteignhead ... 8 SX97
Comrie ... 52 NN72
Congleton ... 30 SJ86
Congresbury ... 14 ST46
Coningsby ... 33 TF25
Conington ... 25 TL18
Conisbrough ... 36 SK59
Coniston ... 38 SD39
Connah's Quay ... 29 SJ26
Connel ... 54 NM93
Conon Bridge ... 60 NH55
Consett ... 45 NZ15
Constantine Bay ... 4 SW87
Contin ... 60 NH45
Conwy ... 29 SH77
Cooden Beach ... 12 TQ70
Cookham ... 16 SU88
Copplestone ... 7 SS70
Copthorne ... 12 TQ33
Corbiere ... 9 JS00
Corbridge ... 45 NY96
Corby Glen ... 32 TF02
Corby ... 25 SP88

Corfe Castle	9	SY98	Crowland	33	TF21	Devizes	15	SU06
Corfe Mullen	10	SY99	Crowlas	4	SW53	Dewsbury	35	SE22
Corgarff	57	NJ20	Crowle	36	SE71	Dhoon	38	SC48
Corhampton	10	SU62	Crowthorne	16	SU86	Diabaig	59	NG75
Corley Ash	24	SP28	Croy	61	NH74	Dibden Purlieu	10	SU40
Cornhill	62	NJ55	Croyde	6	SS43	Didcot	16	SU58
Cornhill-on-Tweed	49	NT83	Croydon	17	TQ36	Dinas Mawddwy	29	SH81
Cornwood	5	SX65	Cruden Bay	63	NK03	Dingwall	60	NH55
Corpach	55	NN07	Cruden Bay	63	NK13	Dinnet	57	NO40
Corran	59	NG80	Crudgington	30	SJ61	Dinnington	32	SK58
Corrie	46	NS04	Crudwell	15	ST99	Dippen	46	NR73
Corris	28	SH70	Crugybar	21	SN63	Dirleton	48	NT58
Corse Lawn	23	SO83	Crumlin	14	ST29	Diseworth	31	SK42
Corsham	15	ST87	Cuckfield	12	TQ32	Disley	31	SJ98
Corsley	15	ST84	Cuckney	32	SK57	Diss	27	TM17
Corstorphine	48	NT17	Cuddington	30	SJ57	Ditchling	12	TQ31
Corton	27	TM59	Cudworth	36	SE30	Ditton Priors	23	SO68
Corwen	29	SJ04	Cuffley	17	TL30	Dobwalls	5	SX26
Coryton	12	TQ78	Culcheth	34	SJ69	Docking	26	TF73
Cosham	11	SU60	Cullen	62	NJ56	Doddington	49	NT93
Coshieville	52	NN74	Cullercoats	45	NZ37	Doddington	26	TL39
Cossington	32	SK61	Cullingworth	35	SE03	Doddington	13	TQ95
Cottenham	18	TL46	Cullivoe	63	HP50	Dodworth	35	SE30
Cottered	18	TL32	Cullompton	7	ST00	Dogmersfield	16	SU75
Cottesmore	32	SK91	Culmstock	7	ST11	Dolfor	22	SO18
Cottingham	25	SP89	Culnacnoc	58	NG57	Dolgellau	28	SH71
Coulport	51	NS28	Culross	48	NS98	Dollar	52	NS99
Coulsdon	12	TQ35	Cumbernauld	47	NS77	Dolphinton	48	NT14
Coundon	40	NZ99	Cuminestown	62	NJ75	Dolwyddelan	28	SH75
Countesthorpe	25	SP59	Cummingston	61	NJ16	Doncaster	36	SE50
Coupar Angus	53	NO23	Cumnock	47	NS51	Donington	33	TF23
Cove	64	NG89	Cumrew	44	NY55	Donnington	23	SJ60
Cove	51	NS28	Cupar	53	NO31	Dorchester	9	SY69
Coventry	24	SP37	Cwm Ystwyth	22	SN77	Dorchester-on-Thames	16	SU59
Coverack	4	SW71	Cwm-y-Glo	28	SH56	Dores	60	NH53
Cowbridge	14	SS97	Cymbach	14	SO00	Dorking	11	TQ14
Cowdenbeath	53	NT19	Cwmbran	14	ST29	Dormington	23	SO54
Cowes	10	SZ49	Cymmer	21	SS89	Dornie	59	NG82
Cowfold	11	TQ22	Cynwyl Elfed	21	SN32	Dornoch	61	NH78
Cowley	16	SP50				Dorridge	24	SP17
Cowley	17	TQ08				Douglas	38	SC37
Coxhoe	45	NZ33	Dagenham	18	TQ58	Douglas	47	NS83
Coxwold	40	SE57	Dailly	42	NS20	Douglas	38	SC37
Coylumbridge	56	NH91	Dairy	35	NS24	Dounby	67	HY22
Coylton	47	NS41	Dalbeattie	43	NX86	Doune	52	NN70
Crackington Haven	6	SX19	Dale	20	SM80	Dover	13	TR34
Cradley Heath	24	SO98	Dalgety Bay	48	NT18	Dovercourt	19	TM23
Cragg	35	SE02	Dalkeith	48	NT36	Down Thomas	5	SX55
Craigellachie	61	NJ24	Dallas	61	NJ15	Downderry	5	SX35
Craighouse	50	NR56	Dalmally	55	NN12	Downton	10	SU12
Craignure	54	NM73	Dalmellington	47	NS40	Drakemyre	47	NS25
Craigrothie	53	NO31	Dalry	43	NX68	Draycott	31	SK43
Crail	53	NO60	Dalrymple	47	NS31	Drimnin	54	NM55
Cramlington	45	NZ27	Dalston	44	NY35	Droitwich	23	SO86
Cramond Foreshore	48	NT27	Dalton	43	NY17	Dronfield	31	SK37
Cranborne	10	SU01	Dalwhinnie	56	NN68	Droxford	10	SU61
Cranbrook	12	TQ73	Darenth	12	TQ57	Drumbeg	65	NC13
Cranfield	25	SP94	Daresbury	30	SJ58	Drumclog	47	NS63
Cranleigh	11	TQ03	Darlaston	24	SO99	Drummore	42	NX13
Crantock	4	SW76	Darley Dale	31	SK26	Drumnadrochit	60	NH53
Cranwell	33	TF04	Darlington	40	NZ21	Drybrook	23	SO61
Crapstone	5	SX56	Darrington	36	SE41	Drymen	52	NS48
Crathorne	40	NZ40	Dartford	12	TQ57	Duddington	25	SK90
Craven Arms	23	SO48	Dartmeet	5	SX67	Dudley	24	SO99
Crawford	48	NS92	Dartmouth	8	SX85	Duffield	31	SK34
Crawfordjohn	47	NS82	Darton	35	SE31	Dufftown	61	NJ33
Crawley	12	TQ23	Darvel	47	NS53	Duirinish	59	NG73
Crayford	12	TQ57	Darwen	34	SD62	Dulnain Bridge	61	NH92
Creagorry	64	NF74	Datchet	12	SU97	Dulverton	7	SS92
Crediton	7	SS80	Davenham	30	SJ67	Dumbarton	51	NS37
Creetown	42	NX45	Daventry	25	SP56	Dumfries	43	NX97
Cregneish	38	SC16	Daviot	60	NH73	Dunbar	49	NT67
Cressage	23	SJ50	Dawley	30	SJ60	Dunbeath	67	ND12
Crewe	30	SJ75	Dawlish	8	SX97	Dunblane	52	NN70
Crewkerne	9	ST40	Deal	13	TR35	Dunchurch	24	SP47
Crianlarich	55	NN32	Deanston	52	NN60	Dundee	53	NO43
Criccieth	28	SH53	Debenham	19	TM16	Dundonnell	59	NH08
Crick	25	SP57	Deddington	24	SP43	Dundry	14	ST56
Crickhowell	22	SO21	Dedham	19	TM03	Dunfermline	52	NT08
Cricklade	15	SU09	Deepcut	16	SU95	Dunholme	32	TF07
Crieff	52	NN82	Deeping St James	33	TF10	Dunkeld	52	NO04
Crinan	51	NR79	Deeping St Nicholas	33	TF21	Dunkirk	13	TR05
Crockernwell	8	SX79	Deganwy	27	SH77	Dunnet	67	ND27
Crocketford	43	NX87	Delabole	5	SX08	Dunning	52	NO01
Croft-on-Tees	40	NZ20	Delph	35	SD90	Dunoon	51	NS17
Cromarty	61	NH76	Denaby	35	SK49	Dunragit	42	NX15
Cromdale	61	NJ02	Denbigh	29	SJ06	Duns	49	NT75
Cromer	27	TG24	Denby Dale	35	SE20	Dunscore	43	NX88
Cronton	34	SJ48	Denham	17	TQ08	Dunsfold	11	TQ03
Crook	45	NZ13	Denholm	48	NT51	Dunsop Bridge	34	SD64
Crookham Village	11	SU75	Denholme	35	SE03	Dunstable	17	TL02
Crooklands	39	SD58	Dennington	19	TM26	Dunster	7	SS94
Crosby	38	SC37	Denny	52	NS88	Duntocher	47	NS47
Crosby	34	SJ39	Denshaw	35	SD91	Dunton Green	12	TQ55
Crosby-on-Eden	44	NY45	Dent	30	SJ78	Duntulm	58	NG47
Cross Hands	21	SN51	Denton	35	SJ99	Dunvegan	58	NG24
Cross-in-Hand	12	TQ52	Derby	31	SK33	Dunwich	27	TM47
Crossmichael	43	NX76	Derbyhaven	38	SC26	Durham	45	NZ24
Crossway Green	23	SO86	Dervaig	54	NM45	Durness	65	NC46
Crosthwaite	39	SD49	Desborough	25	SP88	Duror	55	NM95
Croston	34	SD41	Desford	24	SK40	Dursley	15	ST79
Croughton	24	SP53	Detling	12	TQ75	Duxford	18	TL44
Crowborough	12	TQ53	Devauden	14	ST49	Dyce	57	NJ81
Crowfield	19	TM15	Devil's Bridge	22	SN77	Dyffryn Ardudwy	28	SH52

Dylife	22	SN89
Dymchurch	13	TR12
Dysart	53	NT39
Dyserth	29	SJ07
Eaglescliffe	40	NZ41
Eaglesfield	44	NY27
Eaglesham	47	NS55
Ealing	17	TQ18
Eamont Bridge	39	NY52
Earby	35	SD94
Earl Barton	25	SP86
Earl Shilton	24	SP49
Earlston	48	NT53
Earsdon	45	NZ37
Easdale	50	NM71
Easington	45	NZ44
Easington	41	NZ71
Easington	37	TA41
Easingwold	40	SE56
East Ayton	41	SE98
East Bilney	27	TF91
East Challow	16	SU38
East Cowes	10	SZ59
East Croachy	60	NH62
East Dereham	27	TF91
East Grinstead	12	TQ33
East Harling	27	TL98
East Horndon	18	TQ68
East Horsley	11	TQ05
East Kilbride	47	NS65
East Leake	32	SK52
East Linton	48	NT57
East Lulworth	9	SY88
East Nilney	26	TF91
East Peckham	12	TQ64
East Portlemouth	8	SX73
East Preston	11	TQ00
East Retford	32	SK78
East Rudham	26	TF82
East Wittering	11	SZ79
Eastbourne	12	TV69
Eastchurch	13	TQ97
Eastdean	12	TV59
Easter Skeld	63	HU34
Eastfield	41	TA08
Eastham	30	SJ38
Eastleigh	10	SU41
Eastwood	31	SK44
Eathorpe	24	SP36
Ebbw Vale	14	SO10
Ebchester	45	NZ15
Ecclefechan	43	NY17
Eccles	49	NT74
Eccles	35	SJ79
Eccleshall	30	SJ82
Echt	57	NJ7Q
Edburton	11	TQ21
Edderton	60	NH78
Edenbridge	12	TQ44
Edenhall	44	NY53
Edgeware	17	TQ19
Edinbane	58	NG35
Edinburgh Airport	48	NT17
Edinburgh	48	NT27
Edmonton	17	TQ39
Edmundbyers	45	NZ05
Edwinstowe	32	SK66
Edzell	57	NO56
Egerton	34	SD71
Eggesford	6	SS61
Egglescliffe	40	NZ41
Egglestone	39	NY92
Egham	17	TQ07
Eglingham	49	NU11
Eglwysfach	22	SN69
Eglwyswrw	20	SN13
Egremont	38	NY01
Egton	41	NZ80
Elan	22	SN96
Elberton	15	ST68
Elcot	16	SU36
Elderslie	51	NS46
Elgin	61	NJ26
Elgol	58	NG51
Elie	53	NO40
Elland	35	SE12
Ellesmere Port	30	SJ47
Ellesmere	30	SJ43
Ellingham	27	TM39
Ellon	63	NJ93
Elmstead Market	19	TM02
Elsdon	45	NY99
Elstree	17	TQ19
Elterwater	39	NY30
Eltisley	18	TL25
Elton	25	TL09
Elveden	26	TL88
Elwick	45	NZ43
Ely	26	TL58
Embleton	49	NU22
Embo	66	NH89
Empingham	32	SK90
Emsworth	11	SU70
Endon	31	SJ95
Enfield	17	TQ39
Ennerdale Bridge	38	NY01
Entercommon	40	NZ30
Epping	18	TL40
Epsom	17	TQ26
Epworth	36	SE70
Erdington	24	SP19
Eriboll	65	NC45
Eriska	54	NM94
Erith	12	TQ57
Ermington	5	SX65
Errogie	60	NH52
Erskine	47	NS47
Ervie	42	NW96
Erwood	22	SO04
Esher	17	TQ16
Eskdale Green	38	NY10
Eskdalemuir	44	NY29
Ettington	24	SP24
Ettrickbridge	48	NT32
Evanton	60	NH56
Evercreech	15	ST63
Evershot	9	ST50
Eversley	16	SU76
Evesham	24	SP04
Ewell	17	TQ26
Ewen	15	SU09
Ewhurst	11	TQ04
Ewloe	29	SJ26
Ewyas Harrold	23	SO32
Exbourne	6	SS60
Exebridge	7	SS92
Exeter	8	SX99
Exford	7	SS83
Exmouth	8	SY08
Eye	25	TF20
Eye	27	TM17
Eyemouth	49	NT96
Eynsgam	16	SP40
Fairbourne	28	SH61
Fairford	15	SP10
Fairlie	46	NS25
Fakenham	26	TF93
Faldingworth	33	TF08
Falfield	15	ST69
Falkirk	52	NS87
Falkland	53	NO20
Falmouth	4	SW83
Far Sawrey	39	SD39
Fareham	10	SU50
Faringdon	15	SU29
Farlington	10	SU60
Farnborough	16	SU85
Farnham Common	17	SU98
Farnham	11	SU84
Farningham	12	TQ56
Farnworth	35	SD70
Faringdon	16	SU29
Farrington Gurney	15	ST65
Farthing Corner	12	TQ86
Faugh	44	NY55
Faversham	13	TR06
Fawley	10	SU40
Fazeley	24	SK20
Fearnan	52	NN74
Felbridge	12	TQ33
Felixstowe	19	TM23
Felling	45	NZ26
Felmingham	27	TG12
Feltham	17	TQ17
Felton	45	NU10
Feltwell	26	TL79
Fenny Bentley	31	SK14
Fenny Bridges	8	SY19
Fenny Compton	24	SP45
Fenny Drayton	24	SP39
Fenstanton	18	TL36
Fenwick	47	NS44
Feock	4	SW83
Fermain Bay	4	GN00
Ferndown	10	SU00
Ferness	61	NH94
Ferrybridge S A	36	SE42
Ferryhill	45	NZ23
Fettercairn	57	NO67
Ffestiniog	28	SH74
Filey	41	TA18
Fillongley	24	SP28
Finchingfield	18	TL63
Finchley	17	TQ29
Findhorn	61	NJ06
Findochty	62	NJ46
Findon	11	TQ10
Finedon	25	SP97
Finningham	19	TM06
Finstown	67	HY31
Fintry	52	NS68
Fionnphort	54	NM32
Fir Tree	45	NZ13
Firth	60	NH76
Fishbourne	10	SZ59
Fishguard	20	SM93
Fittleworth	11	TQ0L
Five Oaks	9	JS00
Five Oaks	11	TQ02
Fivehead	14	ST32
Fladbury	24	SO94
Flamborough	41	TA27
Flax Bourton	14	ST56
Fleet	16	SU85
Fleetwood	34	SD34
Flimby	43	NY03
Flimwell	12	TQ73
Flint	29	SJ27
Flitwick	25	TL03
Flockton	35	SE21
Flodigarry	58	NG47
Flore	25	SP66
Fochabers	61	NJ35
Folkestone	13	TR23
Folly Gate	6	SX59
Fontmell Magna	9	ST81
Fontwell	11	SU90
Ford	51	NM80
Ford	15	ST87
Forden	23	SJ20
Fordingbridge	10	SU11
Fordoun	57	NO77
Fordwich	13	TR15
Forest Row	12	TQ43
Forfar	53	NO45
Formby	34	SD30
Forres	61	NJ05
Forsinard	66	NC84
Fort Augustus	60	NH30
Fort William	55	NN17
Forteviot	52	NO01
Forth	47	NS95
Fortingall	52	NN74
Forton S A	39	SD46
Forton	34	SD45
Fortrose	60	NH75
Fossebridge	15	SPO3
Four Marks	11	SU63
Four Mile Bridge	28	SH27
Fourwinds	5	SX17
Fowey	5	SX15
Fownhope	23	SO53
Foyers	60	NH42
Fraddam	4	SW53
Fraddon	4	SW95
Fradley	31	SK11
Framlingham	19	TM26
Frampton Cotterell	15	ST68
Frimwellgate Moor	45	NZ24
Fraserburgh	63	NJ96
Freckenham	26	TL67
Freckleton	34	SD42
Freshwater	10	SZ38
Freswick	67	ND36
Freuchie	53	NO20
Fridaythorpe	41	SE85
Frimley	16	SU85
Frinton-on-Sea	19	TM21
Friockheim	53	NO54
Frizington	38	NY01
Frodsham	30	SJ57
Frome	15	ST74
Froncylite	29	SJ24
Fulletby	33	TF27
Furnace	51	NN00
Furnace	51	NS09
Fyfield	16	SU49
Fyvie	62	NJ73
Gailey	30	SJ91
Gainsborough	36	SK88
Gairloch	59	NG87
Gairlochy	55	NN18
Galashiels	48	NT43
Galgate	39	SD45
Galston	47	NS43
Gamlingay	18	TL25
Ganllwyd	28	SH72
Garboldisham	27	TM08
Garelochhead	51	NS29
Garforth	36	SE43
Gargrave	35	SD95
Garlieston	42	NX44
Garlogie	57	NJ70
Garn Dolbenmaen	28	SH44
Garnant	21	SN61
Garrigill	44	NY74
Garstang	34	SD44
Garth	22	SN94
Garthmyl	22	SO19
Garve	60	NH36
Gatehouse of Fleet	43	NX55
Gateshead	45	NZ26
Gatwick	12	TQ24
Gaydon	24	SP35
Gedney Drove End	33	TF42
Gerrards Cross	17	TQ08

Place	Map	Grid
Giffnock	47	NS55
Gifford	48	NT56
Gigha Island	46	NR64
Gillan	4	SW72
Gillingham	15	ST82
Gillingham	12	TQ76
Gilmerton	52	NN82
Gilmerton	48	NT26
Gilwern	23	SO21
Girvan	42	NX19
Gisburn	35	SD84
Gittistiam	8	SY19
Glamis	53	NO34
Glanton	49	NU01
Glapwell	32	SK46
Glasbury	22	SO13
Glasgow Airport	51	NS46
Glasgow	47	NS56
Glastonbury	14	ST53
Glenbarr	46	NR63
Glenborrodale	54	NM66
Glenbrittle	58	NG42
Glencaple	43	NX96
Glencarse	53	NO12
Glencoe	55	NN15
Gleneagles	52	NN90
Gleneig	59	NG81
Glenfarg	53	NO11
Glenfinnan	54	NM98
Glenkindie	57	NJ41
Glenluce	42	NX15
Glenmaye	38	SC27
Glenridding	39	NY31
Glenrothes	53	NO20
Glenshee	56	NO16
Glenshiel	59	NG91
Glinton	33	TF10
Glossop	35	SK09
Gloucester	23	SO81
Glyn Ceiriog	29	SJ23
Glyn Neath	21	SN80
Glyncorrwg	21	SS89
Goathland	41	NZ80
Gobowen	29	SJ33
Godalming	11	SU94
Godmanchester	25	TL27
Godshill	10	SZ58
Godstone	12	TQ35
Golant	5	SX15
Golspie	66	NH89
Goodrich	23	SO51
Goodrington	8	SX86
Goodwick	20	SM93
Goodwood	11	SU81
Goole	36	SE72
Gordon	49	NT64
Gorey	9	JS00
Goring	16	SU68
Goring-by-Sea	11	TQ10
Gorleston on Sea	27	TG50
Gorseinon	21	SS59
Gosberton	33	TF23
Gosforth	38	NY00
Gosforth	45	NZ26
Gosport	10	SZ69
Goudhurst	12	TQ73
Gowerton	21	SS59
Grain	13	TQ87
Gramisdale	64	NF85
Grandes Rocques	9	GN00
Grands Chemins	9	IS00
Grandtully	52	NN95
Grange	38	NY21
Grange-over-Sands	39	SD47
Grangemouth	52	NS98
Grangetown	40	NZ52
Grantham	32	SK93
Grantown-on-Spey	61	NJ02
Grantshouse	49	NT86
Grasmere	39	NY30
Grassington	40	SE06
Graveley	18	TL22
Gravesend	12	TQ67
Grays	12	TQ67
Great Asby	39	NY61
Great Ayton	40	NZ51
Great Barr	24	SP09
Great Bedwyn	16	SU26
Great Bentley	19	TM12
Great Bircham	26	TF73
Great Blakenham	19	TM15
Great Bookham	17	TQ15
Great Bridgeford	30	SJ82
Great Chesterford	18	TL54
Great Cumbrae	46	NS15
Great Driffield	41	TA05
Great Dunmow	18	TL62
Great Gidding	25	TL18
Great Glen	25	SP69
Great Haywood	31	SJ92
Great Kimble	16	SP80
Great Langdale	38	NY30
Great Leighs	18	TL71
Great Milton	16	SP60
Great Missenden	16	SP80
Great Ponton	32	SK93
Great Shelford	18	TL45
Great Staughton	25	TL16
Great Torrington	6	SS41
Great Wakering	19	TO98
Great Wilbraham	18	TL55
Great Witchingham	27	TG01
Great Witley	23	SO76
Great Yarmouth	27	TG50
Great Yeldham	18	TL73
Greatstone-on-Sea	13	TR02
Green Hammerton	40	SE45
Greenfield	35	SD90
Greenfield	29	SJ17
Greenford	17	TQI8
Greenhead	44	NY66
Greenlaw	49	NT74
Greenloaning	52	NN80
Greenock	51	NS27
Gretland	35	SE02
Greta Green	40	NZ01
Greta Bridge	40	NY36
Gretna	44	NY36
Greystoke	44	NY43
Grimoldby	37	TF38
Grimsargh	34	SD53
Grimsby	37	TA20
Grimston	26	TF72
Grindleford	31	SK27
Gringley-on-the-Hill	36	SK79
Grizedale	39	SD39
Groby	32	SK50
Groeslon	28	SH45
Gronant	29	SJ08
Grosmont	41	NZ80
Grouville Bay	9	JS00
Guard Bridge	53	NO41
Guildford	11	SU94
Guilsborough	25	SP67
Guilsfield	29	SJ21
Guisborough	40	NZ61
Guiseley	35	SE14
Guist	27	TF92
Guilane	48	NT48
Gunnerside	39	SD99
Gunnislake	5	SX47
Gunthorpe	37	SK64
Gurnard	10	SZ49
Gutcher	63	HU59
Guthrie	53	NO55
Guyhirn	26	TF30
Gwbert-on-Sea	20	SN14
Gweek	4	SW72
Gwernymynydd	29	SJ26
Gwithian	4	SW54
Hackness	41	SE99
Haddenham	16	SP70
Haddenham	26	TL47
Haddington	48	NT57
Haddiscoe	27	TM49
Hadleigh	19	TM04
Hadleigh	18	TQ88
Hadley Wood	17	TQ29
Hadlow	12	TQ64
Hailsham	12	TQ50
Hainault	18	TQ49
Halesowen	24	SO98
Halesworth	27	TM37
Halifax	35	SE02
Halkirk	67	ND15
Halkyn	29	SJ17
Halland	12	TQ41
Hallworthy	5	SX18
Halstead	18	TL83
Halwell	8	SX75
Ham Street	13	TR03
Hamble	10	SU40
Hambleton	36	SE53
Hamilton	47	NS75
Hamnavoe	63	HU33
Hampson Green	34	SD56
Hampstead Norreys	16	SU57
Hampsthwaite	40	SE25
Hampton	17	TQ16
Hampton in Arden	24	SP28
Hanchurch	30	SJ84
Handcross	12	TQ22
Handforth	30	SJ88
Handley	30	SJ45
Handsacre	31	SK01
Handsworth	24	SP08
Hanford	30	SJ84
Hanley	30	SJ84
Hanslope	25	SP84
Happisburg	27	TG33
Harborne	24	SP08
Hare Street	18	TL32
Harewood	35	SE34
Harlech	28	SH53
Harleston	27	TM28
Harlosh	58	NG24
Harlow	18	TL41
Harlyn Bay	4	SW87
Harold Wood	18	TQ59
Haroldswick	63	HP61
Harome	40	SE68
Harpenden	17	TL11
Harrogate	35	SE35
Harrold	25	SP95
Harrow	17	TQ18
Harrow Weald	17	TQ19
Hartfield	12	TQ43
Hartford	30	SJ67
Harthill	47	NS96
Hartington	31	SK16
Hartland	6	SS22
Hartlepool	45	NZ53
Hartley Wintney	16	SU75
Harvington	24	SP04
Harwich	19	TM23
Haslemere	11	SU93
Haslingden	35	SD72
Hassocks	12	TQ21
Hastings	12	TQ80
Hatch Beauchamp	8	ST32
Hatfield Heath	18	TL51
Hatfield	36	SE60
Hatfield	17	TL20
Hatherleigh	6	SS50
Hathern	32	SK52
Hathersage	31	SK28
Hatton	31	SK23
Hatton	63	NK03
Haughton-le-Skerne	40	NZ31
Hautes Croix	9	JS00
Havant	11	SU70
Haven St	10	SZ59
Haverfordwest	20	SM91
Haverhill	18	TL64
Hawarden	29	SJ36
Hawes	39	SD88
Haweswater	39	NY41
Hawick	48	NT51
Hawkchurch	9	ST30
Hawkhurst	12	TQ73
Hawkinge	13	TR24
Hawkridge	7	SS83
Hawkshead	39	SD39
Hawnby	40	SE58
Haworth	35	SE03
Haxby	40	SE65
Hay-on-Wye	23	SO24
Haydock	34	SJ59
Haydon Bridge	44	NY86
Hayes	17	TQ08
Hayle	4	SW53
Hayling Island	11	SU70
Hayton	44	NY55
Haytor	8	SX77
Haywards Heath	12	TQ32
Hazel Grove	30	SJ98
Heacham	26	TF63
Headcorn	13	TQ84
Headingley	35	SE23
Heanor	31	SK44
Heathfield	12	TQ52
Heathrow Airport	17	TQ07
Hebburn	45	NZ36
Heckfield	16	SU76
Hebden Bridge	35	SD92
Heckington	33	TF14
Hedge End	10	SU41
Hednesford	31	SK01
Hedon	37	TA12
Heighington	40	NZ22
Helensburgh	51	NS28
Helford	4	SW72
Hellidon	24	SP55
Hellifield	39	SD85
Helmingham	19	TM15
Helmsdale	67	ND01
Helmsley	40	SE68
Helpringham	33	TF14
Helsby	30	SJ47
Helston	4	SW62
Hemel Hempstead	17	TL00
Hemingford Abbots	26	TL27
Hempnall	27	TM29
Hempsted	23	SO81
Hemsby	27	TG41
Hemsworth	36	SE41
Hemyock	7	ST11
Henfield	11	TQ21
Heneade	14	ST22
Henley	19	TM15
Henley on Thames	16	SU78
Henley-in-Arden	24	SP16
Henllan	29	SJ06
Henlow	25	TL13
Henstridge	15	ST72
Hereford	23	SO54
Hermitage	16	SU57
Herne Bay	13	TR16
Herstmonceux	12	TQ61
Hertford Heath	17	TL31

Hertford   Kingseat

Place		
Hertford	17	TL31
Hesketh Bank	34	SD42
Hesleden	45	NZ43
Hessle	37	TA02
Heswall	29	SJ28
Hethersett	27	TG10
Hetton-le-Hole	45	NZ34
Hetton-le-Hole	41	SE79
Heveningham	27	TM37
Heversham	39	SD48
Hewish	14	ST46
Hexham	45	NY96
Hexworthy	5	SX67
Heysham	39	SD46
Heytesbury	15	ST94
Heywood	35	SD81
High Bentham	39	SD66
High Ercall	30	SJ51
High Halden	13	TQ83
High Hesket	44	NY44
High Wycombe	16	SU89
Higham Ferrers	25	SP96
Highampton	6	SS40
Highbridge	14	ST34
Highcliffe	10	SZ29
Higher Penwortham	34	SD52
Higher Town	4	SV91
Highley	23	SO78
Highworth	15	SU29
Hildenborough	12	TQ54
Hill of Fearn	61	NH87
Hillingdon	17	TQ08
Hillington	26	TF72
Hillswick	63	HU27
Hilton	31	SK23
Himley	23	SO89
Hindhead	11	SU83
Hindley	34	SD60
Hindon	15	ST93
Hingham	27	TG00
Hinkley	24	SP49
Hintlesham	19	TM04
Hinton	10	SZ29
Hirwaun	14	SN90
Hitchin	25	TL12
Hockley Heath	24	SP17
Hockliffe	25	SP92
Hoddesdon	18	TL30
Hoddlesden	34	SD72
Hodnet	30	SJ62
Holbeach	33	TF32
Holford	14	ST14
Holkham	26	TF84
Holland-on-Sea	19	TM21
Hollingbourne	13	TQ85
Hollingworth	35	SK09
Hollywood	24	SP07
Holmbury St Mary	11	TQ14
Holme Chapel	35	SD82
Holme-upon-Spalding Moor	36	SE83
Holmes Chapel	30	SJ76
Holmfirth	35	SE10
Holmrook	38	SD09
Holne	8	SX76
Holsworthy	6	SS30
Holt	30	SJ45
Holt	27	TG03
Holy Island	49	NU14
Holyhead	28	SH28
Holyhead	28	SH28
Holywell Green	35	SE01
Holywell	29	SJ17
Homersfield	27	TM28
Honeybourne	24	SP14
Honiley	24	SP27
Honiton	8	ST10
Honley	35	SE11
Hoo	12	TQ77
Hook	15	SU08
Hook	16	SU75
Hope	8	SX63
Hope	31	SK18
Hope under Dinmore	23	SO55
Hopeman	61	NJ16
Hopton-on-Sea	27	TM59
Horley	12	TQ24
Hornby	39	SD56
Horncastle	33	TF26
Hornchurch	18	TQ58
Horndean	11	SU71
Horning	27	TG31
Hornsea	37	TA14
Horrabridge	5	SX57
Horringer	19	TL86
Horsehouse	40	SE07
Horsey	27	TG42
Horsforth	35	SE23
Horsham	11	TQ13
Horsington	15	ST62
Horsley Woodhouse	31	SK34
Horton	8	ST31
Horton-cum-Studley	16	SP51
Horton-in-Ribblesdale	39	SD87
Horwich	34	SD61
Hothfield	13	TQ94
Houbie	63	HU69
Hough Green	30	SJ48
Houghton le Spring	45	NZ35
Houghton-on-the-Hill	25	SK60
Hounslow	17	TQ17
Houton	67	HY30
Hove	12	TQ20
Hovingham	40	SE67
Howcaple	23	SO63
Howden	36	SE72
Howden-le-Wear	45	NZ13
Howton	39	NY41
Howood	47	NS36
Hoylake	34	SJ28
Hoyland Nether	36	SE30
Hucknall	32	SK54
Huddersfield	35	SE11
Hugh Town	4	SV91
Hull	37	TA02
Hullavington	15	ST88
Humberston	25	SK60
Humbie	48	NT46
Hungerford	16	SU36
Hunmanby	41	TA07
Hunstanton	26	TF64
Hunstrete	15	ST66
Hunters Quay	51	NS17
Huntingdon	25	TL27
Huntley	23	SO71
Huntly	62	NJ53
Hurley	16	SU88
Hurliness	67	ND28
Hurst Green	34	SD63
Hurst Green	12	TQ72
Hurst	16	SU77
Hurstbourne Priors	10	SU44
Hurstbourne Tarrant	16	SU35
Husbands Bosworth	25	SP68
Husborne Crawley	25	SP93
Husinish	64	NA91
Husthwaite	40	SE57
Hutton	34	SD42
Hutton-le-Hole	41	SE79
Huyton	34	SJ49
Hyde	35	SJ99
Hynish	50	NL93
Hythe	10	SU40
Hythe	13	TR13
Ibstock	31	SK41
Ideford	8	SX87
Ilchester	14	ST52
Ilford	18	TQ48
Ilfracombe	6	SS54
Ilkeston	31	SK44
Ilkley	35	SE14
Illingworth	35	SE02
Ilminster	9	ST31
Ilsington	8	SX77
Ilton	9	ST31
Immingham Dock	37	TA11
Immingham	37	TA11
Inchnadamph	65	NC22
Ingatestone	18	TL60
Ingleton	39	SD67
Ingoldisthorpe	26	TF63
Ingoldmells	33	TF56
Injebrek	38	SC38
Inkberrow	24	SP05
Innellan	51	NS17
Innerleithen	48	NT33
Insch	62	NJ62
Insh	56	NH80
Instow	6	SS43
Inverallochy	63	NK06
Inveraray	51	NN00
Inverey	56	NO08
Inverfarigaig	60	NH52
Invergarry	55	NH30
Invergordon	60	NH66
Inverkeilor	53	NO64
Inverkeithing	48	NT18
Inverkip	51	NS27
Inverkirkaig	65	NC01
Invermoriston	60	NH41
Inverness	60	NH64
Invershin	66	NH59
Inversnaid	51	NN30
Inverurie	56	NJ72
Ipswich	19	TM14
Irby	29	SJ28
Irlam	34	SJ79
Ironbridge	23	SJ60
Irthlingborough	25	SP97
Irvine	47	NS33
Isle of Whithorn	42	NX43
Isle Ornsay	59	NG71
Isleworth	17	TQ17
Iver Heath	17	TQ08
Iver	17	TQ08
Ivinghoe	17	SP91
Ivybridge	5	SX65
Iwade	13	TQ96
Ixworth	27	TL97
Jackton	47	NS55
Jedburgh	49	NT62
Jerbourg	48	GN00
John O'Groats	67	ND37
Johnshaven	57	NO76
Johnstone Bridge	43	NY09
Johnstone	51	NS46
Johnston	20	SM91
Jurby West	38	SC39
Kames	51	NR97
Kegworth	32	SK42
Keighley	35	SE04
Keiss	67	ND36
Keith	62	NJ45
Keld	39	NY80
Kelso	49	NT73
Kelvedon	19	TL81
Kemble	15	ST99
Kemnay	57	NJ71
Kempston Hardwick	25	TL04
Kempston	25	TL04
Kendal	39	SD59
Kenilworth	24	SP27
Kenmore	52	NN74
Kennacraig	51	NR86
Kennet	52	NS99
Kennethmont	62	NJ52
Kennford	8	SX98
Kenninghall	27	TM08
Kensaleyre	58	NG45
Kensworth	25	TL01
Kentallen	55	NN05
Kentisbeare	7	ST00
Kentra	54	NM66
Kerne Bridge	23	SO51
Kessingland	27	TM58
Keswick	38	NY22
Kettering	25	SP87
Kettletoft	67	HY63
Kettlewell	39	SD97
Keynsham	15	ST66
Kibworth Harcourt	25	SP69
Kidderminster	23	SO87
Kidlington	16	SP41
Kidsgrove	30	SJ85
Kidwelly	21	SN40
Kielder	44	NY69
Kilberry	50	NR76
Kilbirnie	47	NS35
Kilburn	40	SE57
Kilchattan	46	NS05
Kilchiaran	50	NR26
Kilchrenan	51	NN02
Kilcreggan	51	NS28
Kildrummy	57	NJ41
Kildwick	35	SE04
Kilfinan	51	NR97
Kilkhampton	6	SS21
Killearn	52	NS58
Killiecrankie	56	NN96
Killin	52	NN53
Kilmacolm	51	NS36
Kilmaluag	58	NG47
Kilmarnock	47	NS43
Kilmartin	51	NR89
Kilmaurs	47	NS44
Kilmelford	51	NM81
Kilmore	58	NG60
Kilmory	50	NR77
Kilnhurst	36	SK49
Kilninver	51	NM82
Kilnsea	37	TA41
Kilnsey	39	SD96
Kilsby	24	SP57
Kilsyth	52	NS77
Kilve	7	ST14
Kilwinning	47	NS34
Kimberley	27	TG00
Kimbolton	25	TL16
Kinbrace	66	NC83
Kinbuck	52	NN70
Kincardine	52	NS98
Kincardine O'Neil	57	NO59
Kinclaven	53	NO13
Kincraig	56	NH80
Kineton	24	SP35
King's Bromley	31	SK11
King's Langley	17	TL00
King's Lynn	26	TF62
King's Mills	26	GN00
Kingham	16	SP22
Kinghorn	48	NT28
Kingsbarns	53	NO51
Kingsbridge	8	SX74
Kingsbury	24	SP29
Kingsclere	16	SU55
Kingsdown	13	TR34
Kingseat	52	NT19

Kingsfold 11 TQ13
Kingsgate 13 TR37
Kingskerswell 8 SX86
Kingsley 30 SJ57
Kingsmead 10 SU51
Kingstanding 24 SP09
Kingsteignton 8 SX87
Kingston Bagpuize 16 SU49
Kingston 61 NJ36
Kingston upon Thames 17 TQ16
Kingswear 8 SX85
Kingswinford 23 SO88
Kington Langley 15 ST97
Kington 23 SO25
Kingussie 56 NH70
Kinloch Hourn 59 NG90
Kinloch Rannoch 52 NN65
Kinlochard 52 NN40
Kinlochbervie 65 NC25
Kinlocheil 55 NM97
Kinlochewe 59 NH06
Kinlochleven 55 NN16
Kinlochmoidart 54 NM77
Kinloss 61 NJ06
Kinnesswood 53 NO10
Kinross 53 NO10
Kintore 57 NJ71
Kippen 52 NS69
Kirby Misperton 41 SE77
Kirby Muxloe 31 SK50
Kirkby Fleetham 40 SE29
Kirkby Lonsdale 39 SD67
Kirkby Stephen 39 NY70
Kirkby-in-Furness 38 SD28
Kirkbymoorside 41 SE68
Kirk Langley 31 SK23
Kirk Michael 38 SC39
Kirkhill 60 NH54
Kirkintilloch 47 NS67
Kirkburton 35 SE11
Kirkby Malzeard 40 SE27
Kirkby 34 SJ49
Kirkby-in-Ashfield 32 SK55
Kirkcaldy 53 NT29
Kirkcolm 42 NX06
Kirkcowan 42 NX36
Kirkcudbright 43 NX65
Kirkham 34 SD43
Kirkhill 60 NH54
Kirkintilloch 47 NS67
Kirkmichael 56 NO06
Kirkmichael 47 NS30
Kirknewton 48 NT16
Kirknewton 49 NT93
Kirkpatrick Fleming 44 NY27
Kirkwall 67 HY41
Kirkwhelpington 45 NY98
Kirriemuir 53 NO35
Kirton-in-Lindsey 36 SK99
Knaresborough 40 SE35
Knebworth 17 TL22
Knighton 23 SO27
Knightwick 23 SO75
Knockan 65 NC21
Knockandhu 61 NJ22
Knockin 29 SJ32
Knocksharry 38 SC28
Knottingley 36 SE52
Knowle 24 SP17
Knowsley 34 SJ49
Knutsford 30 SJ77
Kyle of Lochalsh 59 NG72
Kyleakin 59 NG72
Kylerhea 59 NG72
Kylestrome 65 NC23

L'Eree 65 GN00
L'Etacq 9 JS00
L'Islet 9 GN00
Laceby 37 TA20
Lady Green 34 SD30
Ladybank 53 NO30
Ladykirk 49 NT84
Lagg 50 NR57
Lagg 46 NR92
Laggan 56 NN69
Laide 64 NG99
Lairg 66 NC50
Lamberhurst 12 TQ63
Lambourn 16 SU37
Lamlash 46 NS03
Lamorna Cove 4 SW42
Lampeter 21 SN54
Lamphey 20 SN00
Lamport 25 SP77
Lanark 47 NS84
Lancaster 39 SD46
Lanchester 45 NZ14
Lancing 11 TQ10
Land's End 4 SW32
Landcross 6 SS42
Langbank 51 NS37
Langho 34 SD73
Langholm 44 NY38

Langland Bay 21 SS68
Langley 17 SU07
Langley Mill 31 SK44
Langley Park 45 NZ24
Langport 14 ST42
Langsett 35 SE20
Langstone 14 ST38
Langthwaite 40 NZ00
Langtoft 33 TF11
Langwathby 44 NY53
Lanivet 5 SX06
Lanreath 5 SX15
Lapford 7 SS70
Lapworth 24 SP17
Larbert 52 NS88
Largo Ward 53 NO40
Largs 46 NS25
Larkfield 12 TQ75
Larkhall 47 NS75
Lasswade 48 NT36
Lastingham 41 SE79
Latchingdon 19 TL80
Latheron 67 ND23
Lauder 48 NT54
Laugharne 20 SN31
Launceston 5 SX38
Laurencekirk 57 NO77
Laurieston 43 NX66
Lavenham 19 TL94
Laverstoke 10 SU44
Lawers 52 NN63
Lawshall 19 TL85
Laxey 38 SC48
Laxford Bridge 65 NC24
Laxo 63 HU46
Lazonby 44 NY53
Le Bourg 44 GN00
Le Bourg 9 JS00
Leadburn 48 NT25
Leaden Roding 18 TL51
Leadenham 32 SK95
Leadhills 47 NS81
Lea Marston 24 SP29
Leamington Spa 24 SP36
Leatherhead 17 TQ15
Lechlade 15 SU29
Leckmelm 65 NH19
Ledbury 23 SO73
Ledmore Junction 65 NC21
Lee Mill 5 SX65
Lee 6 SS44
Lee-on-Solent 10 SU50
Leeds 35 SE33
Leedstown 4 SW63
Leek 31 SJ95
Leekbrook 31 SJ95
Leeming Bar 40 SE28
Leicester 25 SK50
Leigh 30 SD60
Leigh 9 ST60
Leigh 12 TQ54
Leigh-on-Sea 19 TQ88
Leighton Buzzard 16 SP92
Leintwardine 23 SO47
Leiston 19 TM46
Leith 48 NT27
Lelant 4 SW53
Lendalfoot 42 NX19
Lenham 13 TQ85
Lennoxtown 47 NS67
Lenwade 27 TG01
Lenzie 47 NS67
Leominster 23 SO45
Lerwick 63 HU44
Les Buttes 9 GN00
Leslie 53 NO20
Leswalt 42 NX06
Letchworth 18 TL23
Letham 53 NO31
Letham 53 NO54
Letterfinlay 55 NN29
Letterston 20 SM92
Leuchars 53 NO42
Leven 53 NO30
Leven 37 TA14
Levens 39 SD48
Lewdown 5 SX48
Lewes 12 TQ41
Leyburn 40 SE19
Leyland 34 SD52
Leysdown-on-Sea 13 TR07
Lichfield 31 SK10
Lifton 5 SX38
Lightwater 17 SU96
Lilliesleaf 48 NT52
Limpley Stoke 15 ST76
Lincoln 32 SK97
Lindford 11 SU83
Lingfield 12 TQ34
Linlithgow 48 NT07
Linslade 16 SP92
Linton 18 TL54
Linwood 51 NS46
Liphook 11 SU83

Liskeard 5 SX26
Liss 11 SU72
Litherland 34 SJ39
Little Berkhampstead 17 TL20
Little Brickhill 25 SP93
Little Chalfont 16 SU99
Little Compton 24 SP23
Little Hulton 34 SD70
Little Langdale 38 NY30
Little Walsingham 27 TF93
Little Weighton 37 SE93
Littleborough 35 SD91
Littlebourne 13 TR25
Littlehampton 11 TQ00
Littleport 26 TL58
Littlestone-on-Sea 13 TR02
Liverpool 34 SJ39
Liversedge 35 SE22
Livingston 48 NT06
Lizard 4 SW71
Llanaelhaearn 28 SH34
Llanaelhaearn 28 SH44
Llanarmon Dyffryn Ceiriog 29 SJ13
Llanarth 21 SN45
Llanbedr 28 SH52
Llanbedr 29 SJ15
Llanberis 28 SH56
Llanbister 22 SO17
Llanbrynmair 22 SH80
Llanbydder 21 SN54
Llanddarog 21 SN51
Llandderfel 29 SH93
Llandegai 28 SH66
Llandegla 29 SJI5
Llandeilo 21 SN62
Llandissilio 20 SN12
Llandogo 14 SO50
Llandovery 21 SN73
Llandrillo 29 SJ03
Llandrindod Wells 22 SO06
Llandudno Junction 29 SH77
Llandudno 29 SH78
Llandybie 21 SN61
Llandyssul 21 SN44
Llanelli 21 SN50
Llanerchymedd 28 SH48
Llanfachraeth 28 SH38
Llanfaethlu 28 SH38
Llanfair Caereinion 29 SJ10
Llanfair Dyffryn 29 SJ15
Llanfair Talhaiarn 29 SH97
Llanfairfechan 28 SH67
Llanfairpwllgwyngyll 28 SH57
Llanfihangel-Nant-Melan 22 SO15
Llanfrothen 28 SH64
Llanfyllin 29 SJ11
Llanfynydd 29 SJ25
Llangadfan 29 SJ01
Llangadog 21 SN72
Llangammarch Wells 22 SN94
Llangefni 28 SH47
Llangennith 21 SS49
Llangernyw 29 SH86
Llangoed 28 SH67
Llangollen 29 SJ24
Llangorse 22 SO12
Llangranog 20 SN35
Llangurig 22 SN97
Llangybi 14 ST39
Llangynidr 22 SO11
Llangynog 29 SJ02
Llanharan 14 ST08
Llanidloes 22 SN98
Llanilar 22 SN67
Llanllwni 21 SN43
Llanon 22 SN56
Llanrhaedr 29 SJ06
Llanrhaedr-ym-Mochnant 29 SJ12
Llanrhidian 21 SS49
Llanrhystud 22 SN56
Llanrwst 29 SH76
Llansamlet 21 SS69
Llansannan 29 SH96
Llansantffraid Glan Conwy 29 SH87
Llansantffraid 22 SN56
Llansantffraid-ym-Mechain 29 SJ22
Llansawel 21 SN63
Llanstephen 21 SN31
Llanteg 20 SN11
Llanthony 23 SO22
Llantrisant 14 ST08
Llantwit Major 7 SS96
Llanuwchllyn 29 SH82
Llanvetherine 23 SO31
Llanvihangel Cruorney 23 SO32
Llanwddyn 29 SJ01
Llanwnda 28 SH45
Llanwrda 21 SN73
Llanwrtyd Wells 22 SN84
Llanymynech 29 SJ22
Llechryd 20 SN24
Llithfaen 28 SH34
Llwyngwril 28 SH50
Llynclys 29 SJ22
Llyswen 22 SO13

Loanhead	48	NT26
Lochailort	54	NM78
Lochaline	54	NM64
Locharbriggs	43	NX98
Lochawe	55	NN03
Lochboisdale	64	NF72
Lochbuie	54	NM62
Lochcarron	59	NG83
Lochdon	54	NM73
Lochearnhead	52	NN52
Lochgair	51	NR99
Lochgelly	53	NT19
Lochgilphead	51	NR88
Lochgoilhead	51	NN20
Lochinver	65	NC02
Lochmaben	43	NY08
Lochranza	46	NR95
Lochwinnoch	47	NS35
Lockerbie	43	NY18
Lochmaddy	58	NF96
Lockton	27	TM39
Loe	5	SX25
Lofthouse	35	SE32
Loftus	41	NZ71
Lolworth	18	TL36
London	17	TQ38
Long Buckby	25	SP66
Long Crendon	16	SK60
Long Eaton	32	SK43
Long Hanborough	16	SP41
Long Melford	19	TL84
Long Preston	39	SD85
Long Stratton	27	TM19
Long Sutton	33	TF42
Longbridge Deverill	15	ST84
Longdown	8	SX89
Longformacus	49	NT65
Longframlington	45	NU10
Longham	10	SZ09
Longhorsley	45	NZ19
Longhoughton	49	NU21
Longmorn	61	NJ25
Longniddry	48	NT47
Longnor	23	SJ40
Longnor	31	SK06
Longridge	34	SD63
Longton	34	SD42
Longton	30	SJ94
Longville	23	SO59
Lossiemouth	61	NJ27
Lostwithiel	5	SX15
Loughborough	32	SK51
Loughor	21	SS59
Loughton	18	TQ49
Louth	33	TF38
Low Eggborough	36	SE52
Lowdham	32	SK64
Lower Barvas	64	NB45
Lower Beeding	11	TQ22
Lower Brailes	24	SP33
Lower Slaughter	24	SP12
Lowestoft	27	TM59
Loweswater	38	NY12
Lowick	49	NU03
Ludborough	37	TF29
Luddenden	35	SE02
Ludgershall	10	SU25
Ludlow	23	SO57
Ludwell	15	ST92
Lugton	47	NS45
Lugwardine	23	SO54
Lumbly	36	SE43
Lumphanan	57	NJ50
Lumsden	57	NJ42
Lunan Bay	53	NO65
Lundin Links	53	NO40
Luss	51	NS39
Luton Airport	17	TL12
Luton	17	TL02
Lutterworth	24	SP58
Lybster	67	ND23
Lydd	13	TR02
Lyddington	25	SP89
Lydford	5	SX58
Lydford-on-Fosse	14	ST53
Lydham	23	SO39
Lydiate	34	SD30
Lydney	15	SO60
Lye	24	SO98
Lyme Regis	9	SY39
Lyminge	13	TR14
Lymington	10	SZ39
Lymm	30	SJ68
Lympsham	14	ST35
Lyndhurst	10	SU20
Lyneham	15	SU07
Lyness	67	ND39
Lynmouth	6	SS74
Lynton	6	SS74
Lytham St Annes	34	SD32
Mablethorpe	33	TF58
Macclesfield	30	SJ97
Macduff	62	NJ76
Machrie	46	NR83
Machrihanish	46	NR62
Machynlleth	22	SH70
Maerdy	14	SS99
Maesteg	21	SS89
Magor	14	ST48
Maiden Bradley	15	ST83
Maiden Newton	9	SY59
Maidencombe	8	SX96
Maidenhead	16	SU88
Maidstone	12	TQ75
Maidwell	25	SP77
Mainsriddle	43	NX95
Maldon	19	TL80
Malham	39	SD86
Mallaig	54	NM69
Mallwyd	29	SH81
Malmesbury	15	ST98
Malpas	30	SJ44
Maltby	36	SK59
Malton	41	SE77
Malvern	23	SO74
Manaccan	4	SW72
Manchester Airport	30	SJ88
Manchester	35	SJ89
Manea	26	TL48
Manorbier	20	SS09
Mansfield	32	SK56
Mansfield Woodhouse	32	SK56
Manston	13	TR36
Mapperley	31	SK44
Marazion	4	SW53
March	26	TL49
Marcham	16	SU49
Marchwiel	30	SJ34
Marchwood	10	SU31
Marden	12	TQ74
Mareham-le-Fen	33	TF26
Maresfield	12	TQ42
Marford	30	SJ35
Margate	13	TR37
Marianglas	28	SH58
Market Bosworth	24	SK40
Market Deeping	33	TF11
Market Drayton	30	SJ63
Market Harborough	25	SP78
Market Rasen	37	TF18
Market Weighton	36	SE84
Markfield	32	SK41
Markham Moor	32	SK77
Markham	14	SO10
Markinch	53	NO30
Markington	40	SE26
Marks Tey	19	TL92
Markyate	17	TL01
Marlborough	15	SU16
Marldon	8	SX86
Marley Hill	45	NZ25
Marlow	16	SU88
Marnhull	9	ST71
Marple	35	SJ98
Marsden	35	SE01
Marshfield	15	ST77
Marske-by-the-Sea	40	NZ62
Marston Magna	15	ST52
Marston Moretaine	25	SP94
Marston Trussell	25	SP68
Martham	27	TG41
Martinhoe	6	SS64
Martock	9	ST41
Marton	40	NZ51
Mary Tavy	5	SX57
Marykirk	57	NO66
Maryport	43	NY03
Masham	40	SE28
Matlock Bath	31	SK25
Matlock	31	SK26
Mattingley	16	SU75
Mauchline	47	NS52
Maughold	38	SC49
Mawdesley	34	SD41
Mawgan Porth	4	SW86
Mawnan Smith	4	SW72
Maybole	47	NS30
Mayfield	12	TQ52
Maypool	8	SX85
Mealsgate	43	NY24
Measham	13	SK31
Medbourne	25	SP79
Meigle	57	NO24
Melksham	15	ST96
Melling	39	SD57
Melmerby	44	NY63
Melmerby	40	SE37
Melrose	48	NT53
Meltham	35	SE01
Melton	36	SE92
Melton Constable	27	TG03
Melton Mowbray	32	SK71
Melvaig	59	NG78
Melvich	66	NC86
Membury	8	ST20
Membury	16	SU37
Memsie	63	NJ96
Menai Bridge	28	SH57
Mere	30	SJ78
Mere	15	ST83
Meriden	24	SP28
Merstham	11	TQ25
Merthyr Tydfil	14	SO00
Messingham	36	SE80
Metheringham	33	TF06
Methlick	62	NJ83
Methven	52	NO02
Methwold	26	TL79
Mevagissey	4	SX04
Mexborough	36	SE40
Micheldever	10	SU53
Mickleton	24	SP14
Mid Yell	63	HU59
Middle Town	4	SV80
Middle Wallop	10	SU23
Middleham	40	SE18
Middlesbrough	40	NZ42
Middleton	50	NL94
Middleton	35	SD80
Middleton Stoney	16	SP52
Middleton-in-Teesdale	39	NY92
Middleton-on-Sea	11	SU90
Middleton-on-the-Wolds	36	SE94
Middlewich	30	SJ76
Midhurst	11	SU82
Midsomer Norton	15	ST65
Midtown Brae	59	NG88
Milborne St Andrew	9	SY89
Mildenhall	26	TL77
Milesmark	52	NT08
Milford Haven	20	SM90
Milford	11	SU94
Milford-on-Sea	10	SZ29
Milland	11	SU82
Millbrook	9	JS00
Millbrook	5	SX45
Millhouse	51	NR97
Millom	38	SD18
Milnathort	53	NO10
Milngavie	47	NS57
Milnrow	35	SD91
Milnthorpe	39	SD48
Milovaig	58	NG15
Milton Abbas	9	ST80
Milton Common	16	SP60
Milton Damerel	6	SS31
Milton Ernest	25	TL05
Milton Keynes	25	SP83
Milton	20	SN00
Milton-on-Stour	15	ST82
Minchinhampton	15	SO80
Minehead	7	SS94
Minera	29	SJ25
Minster Lovell	16	SP31
Minster	13	TR36
Minsterley	23	SJ30
Mintlaw	63	NK04
Mirfield	35	SE21
Miskin	14	ST08
Misterton	36	SK79
Mitcham	17	TQ26
Mitcheldean	23	SO61
Mobberley	30	SJ77
Mochdre	29	SH87
Mochrum	42	NX34
Mockbeggar	10	SU10
Modbury	5	SX65
Moffat	43	NT00
Mold	29	SJ26
Moniaive	43	NX79
Monifieth	53	NO43
Monk Fryston	36	SE52
Monkleigh	6	SS42
Monks Eleigh	19	TL94
Monmouth	23	SO51
Montacute	9	ST41
Montgomery	23	SO29
Montrose	53	NO75
Monymusk	57	NJ61
Moorlinch	14	ST33
Morar	54	NM69
Morden	17	TQ26
Mordiford	23	SO53
Morebattle	49	NT72
Morecambe	39	SD46
Morecombelake	9	SY49
Moreton	34	SJ28
Moreton-in-Marsh	24	SP23
Moretonhampstead	8	SX78
Morfa Nefyn	28	SH24
Morley	35	SE22
Morningside	48	NT27
Morpeth	45	NZ18
Morriston	21	SS69
Mortehoe	6	SS44
Morville	23	SO69
Morwenstow	6	SS21
Mossat	57	NJ41
Mossley	35	SD90
Mostyn	29	SJ18

Motherwell   Pennal

Motherwell	47	NS75
Mottram St Andrew	30	SJ87
Mottram-in-Longdendale	35	SJ99
Moulsford	16	SU58
Mount Hawke	4	SW74
Mountain Ash	14	ST09
Mountsorrel	32	SK51
Mousehole	4	SW42
Moy	60	NH73
Much Birch	23	SO53
Much Hadham	18	TL41
Much Hoole	34	SD42
Much Wenlock	23	SO69
Muchalls	57	NO99
Mudeford	10	SZ19
Muir of Ord	60	NH55
Muirdrum	53	NO53
Muirhead	47	NS67
Muirhead	53	NO33
Muirkirk	47	NS62
Mullion Cove	4	SW61
Mullion	4	SW61
Mumbles	21	SS68
Mundesley-on-Sea	27	TG33
Mundford	26	TL89
Mundon Hill	19	TL80
Mungrisdale	44	NY33
Munslow	23	SO58
Murton	45	NZ34
Musselburgh	48	NT37
Muthill	52	NN81
Mybster	67	ND25
Mytholmroyd	35	SE02
Nailsea	14	ST47
Nailsworth	15	ST89
Nairn	61	NH85
Nannerch	29	SJ16
Nant-Ddu	22	SO01
Nantgarw	14	ST18
Nantwich	30	SJ65
Narberth	20	SN11
Narborough	24	SP59
Narborough	26	TF71
Nayland	19	TL93
Neasham	40	NZ31
Neath	21	SS79
Needham Market	19	TM05
Nefyn	28	SH34
Nelson	35	SD83
Nesscliffe	30	SJ31
Neston	29	SJ27
Nether Broughton	32	SK72
Nethy Bridge	56	NJ02
Nettlebed	16	SU68
Nevern	20	SN03
New Abbey	43	NX96
New Aberdour	62	NJ86
New Blyth	62	NJ85
New Brighton	34	SJ39
New Buckenham	27	TM09
New Cumnock	47	NS61
New Deer	62	NJ84
New Galloway	43	NX67
New Grimsby	4	SV81
New Holland	37	TA02
New Luce	42	NX16
New Malden	17	TQ26
New Mills	31	SK08
New Milton	10	SZ29
New Pitsligo	62	NJ85
New Quay	21	SN35
New Radnor	22	SO26
New Romney	13	TR02
Newark-on-Trent	32	SK75
Newbiggin	39	NY92
Newbiggin-by-the-Sea	45	NZ38
Newbigging	53	NO43
Newbold-upon-Stour	24	SP24
Newborough	28	SH46
Newbridge	48	NT17
Newbridge	16	SP40
Newbridge-on-Wye	22	SO05
Newburgh	63	NJ92
Newburgh	53	NO21
Newburn	45	NZ16
Newbury	16	SU46
Newby Bridge	39	SD38
Newcastle Emlyn	20	SN34
Newcastle upon Tyne Airport	45	NZ17
Newcastle upon Tyne	45	NZ26
Newcastle-under-Lyme	30	SJ84
Newcastleton	44	NY48
Newenden	13	TQ82
Newent	23	SO72
Newgale	20	SM82
Newgate Street	17	TL30
Newhaven	31	SK16
Newhaven	12	TQ40
Newhouse	47	NS76
Newington	13	TQ86
Newlyn	4	SW42
Newmains	47	NS85
Newmarket	18	TL66
Newmill on Teviot	44	NT41
Newnham	23	SO66
Newnham	25	SP84
Newport Pagnell	25	SP84
Newport	30	SJ71
Newport	20	SN03
Newport	14	ST38
Newport	10	SZ48
Newport	18	TL53
Newport-on-Tay	53	NO42
Newquay	4	SW86
Newton Abbot	8	SX87
Newton Aycliffe	40	NZ22
Newton Ferrers	5	SX54
Newton Linford	32	SK51
Newton Poppleford	8	SY08
Newton Solney	31	SK22
Newton St Cyres	8	SX89
Newton Stewart	42	NX46
Newton-le-Willows	34	SJ59
Newton-on-Trent	32	SK87
Newtonmore	61	NH87
Newtown	22	SO19
Newtown	32	SO64
Newtown	10	SU61
Newtown Linford	32	SK51
Newtyle	53	NO24
Neyland	20	SM90
Nigg	61	NH87
Ninfield	12	TQ71
Niton	10	SZ57
Nolton Haven	20	SM81
Norden	35	SD81
Norham	49	NT94
Norman Cross	25	TL19
Normanton	36	SE32
Normanton	32	SK90
North Ballachulish	55	NN06
North Berwick	48	NT58
North Bragar	64	NB24
North Coates	37	TA30
North Elmham	27	TF92
North Erradale	59	NG78
North Ferriby	37	SE92
North Grimston	41	SE86
North Huish	8	SX75
North Kyme	33	TF15
North Molton	7	SS72
North Muskham	32	SK75
North Petherton	14	ST23
North Queensferry	48	NT18
North Roe	63	HU38
North Shields	45	NZ36
North Somercotes	37	TF49
North Stifford	12	TQ68
North Stoke	16	SU68
North Tawton	6	SS60
North Tolsta	64	NB54
North Tuddenham	27	TG01
North Walsham	27	TG23
North Waltham	10	SU54
North Warnborough	11	SU75
North Wootton	9	ST61
Northallerton	40	SE39
Northam	6	SS42
Northampton	25	SP76
Northfleet	12	TQ67
Northiam	12	TQ82
Northleach	24	SP11
Northop Hall	29	SJ26
Northop	29	SJ26
Northwich	30	SJ67
Northwood	17	TQ09
Norton	23	SJ70
Norton St Philip	15	ST75
Norwich	27	TG20
Norwick	63	HP61
Nottingham	32	SK53
Nuneaton	24	SP39
Nunney Catch	15	ST74
Nutfield	12	TQ35
Nutley	12	TQ42
Oadby	25	SK60
Oakengates	30	SJ71
Oakham	32	SK80
Oakley	8	SP61
Oakley	10	SU55
Oakley	25	TL05
Oakworth	35	SE03
Oban	54	NM83
Ochiltree	47	NS52
Ockley	11	TQ14
Odiham	11	SU75
Ogbourne St George	15	SU27
Ogmore-by-Sea	21	SS87
Okehampton	6	SX59
Old Conway	29	SH87
Old Deer	63	NJ94
Old Grimsby	4	SV81
Old Leake	33	TF45
Old Meldrum	62	NJ82
Old Rayne	62	NJ62
Old Sodbury	15	ST78
Old Town	4	SV91
Old Windsor	17	SU97
Oldbury	24	SO98
Oldcotes	36	SK58
Oldham	35	SD90
Ollaberry	63	HU38
Olney	25	SP85
Ombersley	23	SO86
Onchan	38	SC47
Ongar	18	TL50
Onich	55	NN06
Onneley	30	SJ74
Ord	58	NG61
Orford	19	TM45
Orgil	67	HY20
Ormesby	27	TG41
Ormskirk	34	SD40
Orpington	12	TQ46
Orsett	12	TQ68
Osbournby	33	TF03
Osmington	9	SY78
Ossett	35	SE22
Osterley	17	TQ17
Oswaldkirk	40	SE67
Oswaldtwistle	35	SD72
Oswestry	29	SJ22
Otford	12	TQ55
Othery	14	ST33
Otley	35	SE24
Otterburn	45	NY89
Ottery St Mary	8	SY19
Oulton Broad	27	TM59
Oulton Park	30	SJ56
Oulton	36	SE32
Oundle	25	TL08
Outlane	35	SE01
Outwell	26	TF50
Over	30	SJ66
Overseal	31	SK21
Overstrand	27	TG24
Overton	10	SU54
Overton-on-Dee	30	SJ34
Ovington	45	NZ06
Oxenhope	35	SE03
Oxford	16	SP50
Oxted	12	TQ35
Oxton	32	SK65
Paddock Wood	12	TQ64
Padiham	35	SD73
Padstow	4	SW97
Pagham	11	SZ89
Paignton	8	SX86
Painswick	15	SO80
Paisley	47	NS46
Pangbourne	16	SU67
Pannal	35	SE25
Pant-y-Dwr	22	SN97
Par	5	SX05
Parbold	34	SD41
Parkeston Quay	19	TM23
Parkgate	29	SJ27
Parkham	6	SS32
Parkhurst	10	SZ49
Parson Drove	33	TF30
Partick	47	NS56
Partington	34	SJ79
Partridge Green	11	TQ11
Pateley Bridge	40	SE16
Patrick	38	SC28
Patrington	37	TA32
Patterdale	39	NY31
Pathead	48	NT36
Pattingham	23	SO89
Paulton	15	ST65
Peacehaven	12	TQ40
Peasedown St John	15	ST75
Peasmarsh	13	TQ82
Peebles	48	NT24
Peel	38	SC28
Pelynt	5	SX25
Pembridge	23	SO35
Pembroke	20	SM90
Pembroke Dock	20	SM90
Pen-y-gwryd	28	SH65
Penarth	14	ST17
Pencaitland	48	NT46
Pencoed	21	SS98
Pencraig	23	SO52
Pendeen	4	SW33
Pendine	20	SN20
Pendlebury	35	SD70
Pendoggett	4	SX07
Penicuik	48	NT26
Penistone	35	SE20
Penketh	30	SJ58
Penkridge	30	SJ91
Penllergaer	21	SS69
Penmachno	29	SH75
Penmaen	21	SS58
Penmaenmawr	28	SH77
Pennal	22	SH70

Pennard 21 SS58
Penthiwllan 21 SN34
Penrhyndeudraeth 28 SH63
Penrith 44 NY53
Penryn 4 SW73
Pensarn 21 SN41
Penshurst 12 TQ54
Pentewan 4 SX04
Pentre Halkyn 29 SJ27
Pentrefoelas 29 SH85
Penybont 22 SO16
Penybontfawr 29 SJ02
Penyghael 50 NM52
Penygroes 28 SH45
Penzance 4 SW43
Perelle 4 GN00
Perivale 17 TQ18
Perranporth 4 SW75
Perranuthnoe 4 SW52
Perry Bar 24 SP09
Pershore 24 SO94
Perth 52 NO12
Peterborough 25 TL19
Peterchurch 23 SO33
Peterculter 57 NJ80
Peterhead 63 NK14
Peterlee 45 NZ44
Petersfield 11 SU72
Peterstow 23 SO52
Petts Wood 12 TQ46
Petty France 15 ST78
Petworth 11 SU92
Pevensey 12 TQ60
Pewsey 15 SU15
Pickering 41 SE78
Picket Post 10 SU10
Piddletrenthide 9 SY79
Piercebridge 40 NZ21
Pierowall 67 HY44
Pill 14 ST57
Pillerton Priors 24 SP24
Pilning 14 ST58
Pimperne 9 ST90
Pinchbeck 33 TF22
Pinner 17 TQ18
Pinwherry 42 NX18
Pirnmill 46 NR84
Pitcaple 62 NJ72
Pitlochry 52 NN95
Pitmedden 62 NJ82
Pitsea 18 TQ78
Pittenweem 53 NO50
Pleasley 32 SK56
Pleinmont 32 GN00
Plemont 9 JS00
Plockton 59 NG83
Plymouth 5 SX45
Plympton 5 SX55
Pocklington 36 SE84
Podimore 14 ST52
Polbain 64 NB91
Polegate 12 TQ50
Polmont 52 NS97
Polperro 5 SX25
Polruan 5 SX15
Polzeath 4 SW97
Ponders End 17 TQ39
Pontardawe 21 SN70
Pontardulais 21 SN50
Pontefract 36 SE42
Ponteland 45 NZ17
Ponterwyd 22 SN78
Pontesbury 30 SJ30
Pontfadog 29 SJ23
Pontllanfraith 14 ST19
Pontnewydd 14 ST29
Pontrhydfendigaid 22 SN76
Pontrilas 23 SO32
Pontyates 21 SN40
Pontyberem 21 SN51
Pontypool 14 SO20
Pontypridd 14 ST09
Pool-in-Wharfedale 35 SE24
Poole 10 SZ09
Poolewe 59 NG88
Pooley Bridge 39 NY42
Porlock 7 SS84
Porlock Weir 7 SS84
Port Appin 54 NM94
Port Askaig 50 NR46
Port Charlotte 50 NR25
Port Ellen 50 NR34
Port Erin 38 SC16
Port Eynon 21 SS48
Port Glasgow 51 NS37
Port Henderson 59 NG77
Port Isaac 4 SW98
Port Logan 42 NX04
Port of Menteith 52 NN50
Port of Ness 64 NB56
Port Soderick 38 SC37
Port St Mary 38 SC26
Port Talbot 21 SS78
Port William 42 NX34

Portbury 14 ST57
Portchester 10 SU60
Portdinorwic 28 SH56
Portelet Bay 9 JS00
Portgaverne 4 SX08
Porth 14 ST09
Porthcawl 21 SS87
Porthkerry 7 ST06
Porthleven 4 SW62
Porthmadog 28 SH53
Porthtowan 4 SW64
Porthyrhyd 21 SN51
Portishead 14 ST47
Portknockie 62 NJ46
Portland 9 SY67
Portlethen 57 NO99
Portloe 4 SW93
Portmahomack 61 NH98
Portnacroish 55 NM94
Portnahaven 50 NR15
Portpatrick 42 NX05
Portreath 4 SW64
Portree 58 NG44
Portscatho 4 SW83
Portslade-by-Sea 12 TQ20
Portsmouth 11 SZ69
Portsoy 62 NJ56
Portwrinkle 5 SX35
Postcombe 16 SU79
Pott Shrigley 31 SJ97
Potter Heigham 27 TG41
Potters Bar 17 TL20
Potton 18 TL24
Poulton-le-Flyde 23 SO33
Poundsgate 8 SX77
Powburn 49 NU01
Powfoot 43 NY16
Powick 23 SO85
Powmill 52 NT09
Powmill 52 NT09
Poynton 30 SJ98
Praa Sands 4 SW52
Praze-an-Beeble 4 SW63
Prees Health 30 SJ53
Preesall 34 SD34
Prenteg 28 SH54
Prescot 34 SJ49
Prestatyn 29 SJ08
Prestbury 30 SJ87
Presteigne 23 SO36
Preston Gubbals 30 SJ41
Preston 49 NT75
Preston 34 SD53
Prestwich 35 SD80
Prestwick 47 NS32
Princes Risborough 16 SP80
Princethorpe 24 SP47
Princetown 5 SX57
Prudhoe 45 NZ06
Puckeridge 18 TL32
Puddletown 9 SY79
Pudsey 35 SE23
Pulborough 11 TQ01
Pumsaint 21 SN64
Purfleet 12 TQ57
Purley 12 TQ36
Purton 15 SU08
Pwllheli 28 SH73
Pyle 21 SS88

Queen's Park 47 NS56
Queenborough 13 TQ97
Queensbury 35 SE13
Queensferry 29 SJ36
Quendon 18 TL53
Quorn 32 SK51

Raasay 58 NG53
Radcliffe 35 SD70
Radcliffe-on-Trent 32 SK63
Radlett 17 TL10
Radstock 15 ST65
Radwinter 18 TL63
Rafford 61 NJ05
Raglan 14 SO40
Rainford 34 SD40
Rainham 12 TQ58
Rainhill 34 SJ49
Rame 4 SW73
Ramsbottom 35 SD71
Ramsey 38 SC49
Ramsey 26 TL28
Ramsey 19 TM23
Ramsgate 13 TR36
Ramsgill 40 SE17
Rangemore 31 SK12
Rangeworthy 15 ST68
Rannoch Station 55 NN45
Ranworth 27 TG31
Rapness 67 HY54
Rattray 53 NO14

Ravenglass 38 SD09
Ravenscar 40 NE99
Ravenstonedale 39 NY70
Rawmarsh 38 SK49
Rawreth 18 TQ79
Rawtenstall 35 SD82
Rayleigh 18 TQ89
Read 35 SD73
Reading 16 SU77
Rearsby 32 SK61
Reay 66 NC96
Red Row 45 NZ29
Red Wharf Bay 28 SH58
Redbourn 17 TL11
Redbrook 30 SJ54
Redcar 40 NZ62
Redditch 24 SP06
Redhill 12 TQ25
Redland 67 HY32
Redmile 32 SK73
Redruth 4 SW64
Reedham 27 TG40
Reepham 27 TG02
Reeth 40 SE09
Reiff 64 NB91
Reigate 12 TQ25
Reighton 41 TA17
Rempstone 32 SK52
Renfrew 47 NS56
Renishaw 31 SK47
Resolven 21 SN80
Retford 32 SK78
Rettendon 18 TQ79
Reynoldston 21 SS49
Rhayader 22 SN96
Rhiconich 65 NC25
Rhoose 7 ST06
Rhos 21 SN33
Rhos-on-Sea 29 SH88
Rhosneigr 28 SH37
Rhossilli 21 SS48
Rhu 51 NS28
Rhubodach 51 NS07
Rhuddlan 29 SJ07
Rhydowen 21 SN44
Rhyd-ddu 28 SH55
Rhyl 29 SJ08
Rhymney 14 SO10
Rhynie 62 NJ42
Ribchester 34 SD63
Richard's Castle 23 SO46
Richmond 40 NZ10
Richmond upon Thames 17 TQ17
Rickmansworth 17 TQ09
Ridsdale 45 NY98
Rillington 41 SE87
Ringford 43 NX65
Ringsall 17 SP91
Ringwood 10 SU10
Ripley 40 SE26
Ripley 31 SK45
Ripley 17 TQ05
Ripon 40 SE37
Ripple 23 SO83
Ripponden 35 SE01
Risca 14 ST29
Risegate 33 TF22
Riseley 25 TL06
Rishton 34 SD73
Risley 31 SK43
Roadhead 44 NY57
Roberton 47 NS92
Robertsbridge 12 TQ72
Robeston Wathen 20 SN01
Robin Hood's Bay 41 NZ90
Rocester 31 SK13
Rochdale 35 SD81
Rochester 44 NY89
Rochester-upon-Medway 12 TQ76
Rochford 19 TQ89
Rock Ferry 34 SJ38
Rock 4 SW97
Rockbeare 8 SY09
Rockcliffe 43 NX85
Rockingham 25 SP89
Roewen 28 SH77
Rogart 66 NC70
Rogerstone 14 ST28
Rolvenden 13 TQ83
Romaldkirk 39 NY92
Romford 18 TQ58
Romsey 10 SU32
Romsley 24 SO97
Rookhope 45 NY94
Rooksbridge 14 ST35
Ropley 11 SU63
Rosebank 47 NS84
Rosedale Abbey 41 SE79
Rosehall 65 NC40
Rosehearty 63 NH75
Rosemarkie 60 NH75
Rose-on-Wye 23 SO52
Rossett 30 SJ35
Rossington 36 SK69

Rosthwaite	38	NY21	Saxby	32	SK81	Shoreham-by-Sea	11	TQ20	
Rosyth	48	NT18	Saxmundham	19	TM36	Shorwell	10	SZ48	
Rothbury	45	NU00	Saxthorpe	27	TG13	Shotley	19	TM23	
Rotherham	36	SK49	Scalasaig	50	NR39	Shottisham	19	TM34	
Rotherwick	16	SU75	Scalby	41	TA09	Shrawley	23	SO86	
Rothes	61	NJ24	Scalloway	63	HU43	Shrewsbury	30	SJ41	
Rothesay	51	NS06	Scampton	32	SK97	Shrewton	15	SU04	
Rothley	32	SK51	Scarborough	41	TA08	Shrivenham	15	SU28	
Rothwell	35	SE32	Scarinish	50	NM04	Shurdington	24	SO91	
Rothwell	25	SP88	Scarisbrick	34	SD31	Sible Hedingham	18	TL73	
Rottingdean	12	TQ30	Scarista	58	NG09	Sibsey	33	TF35	
Roughton	27	TG23	Scawby	36	SE90	Sibson	24	SK30	
Rousdon	8	SY29	Scole	27	TM17	Sidcup	12	TQ47	
Row	5	SX07	Sconser	58	NG53	Sidmouth	8	SY18	
Rowardennan	51	NS39	Scopwick	33	TF05	Silchester	16	SU66	
Rowen	28	SH77	Scorton	40	NZ20	Silloth	43	NY15	
Rowlands Castle	11	SU71	Scotch Corner	40	NZ20	Silver End	18	TL81	
Rowlands Gill	45	NZ15	Scots' Gap	45	NZ08	Silverdale	39	SD47	
Rowley Regis	24	SO98	Scourie	67	NC14	Silverstone	25	SP64	
Rowsley	31	SK26	Scrabster	67	ND17	Silverton	7	SS90	
Rowstock	16	SU48	Scunthorpe	36	SE81	Simonsbath	7	SS73	
Roxburgh	49	NT63	Sea Palling	27	TG41	Singleton	11	SU81	
Roy Bridge	55	NN28	Seaford	12	TV49	Sittingbourne	13	TQ96	
Royston	36	SE31	Seaham	45	NZ44	Six Mile Bottom	18	TL55	
Royston	18	TL34	Seahouses	49	NU23	Skaill	67	HY50	
Royton	35	SD90	Seale	11	SU84	Skeabost Bridge	58	NG44	
Rozel Bay	9	JS00	Seamer	41	TA08	Skegness	33	TF56	
Ruabon	29	SJ34	Seamill	46	NS14	Skellow	36	SE51	
Ruan High Lanes	4	SW94	Seascale	38	NY00	Skelmersdale	34	SD40	
Ruan Minor	4	SW71	Seathwaite	38	SD29	Skelmorlie	51	NS16	
Rubery	24	SO97	Seatoller	38	NY21	Skenfrith	23	SO42	
Rudgwick	11	TQ03	Seaton Burn	45	NZ27	Skewen	21	SS79	
Rudston	41	TA06	Seaton Carew	40	NZ52	Skipness	46	NR95	
Rufford	34	SD41	Seaton	8	SY29	Skipsea	41	TAI5	
Rugby	24	SP57	Seaview	11	SZ69	Skipton	35	SD90	
Rugeley	31	SK01	Sedbergh	39	SD69	Slaidburn	34	SD75	
Ruislip	17	TQ08	Sedgeberrow	24	SP03	Slaithwaite	35	SE01	
Rumney	14	ST27	Sedgebrook	32	SK83	Slamannan	47	NS87	
Runcorn	30	SJ58	Sedgefield	40	NZ32	Slapton	8	SX84	
Rushden	25	SP96	Sedgemoor S A	14	ST35	Sleaford	33	TF04	
Rushlake Green	12	TQ61	Sedgley	24	SO99	Sledmere	41	SE96	
Rushyford	40	NZ22	Sedlescombe	12	TQ71	Sliddery	46	NR92	
Rusper	11	TQ23	Selborne	11	SU73	Sligachan	58	NG43	
Rustington	11	TQ00	Selby	36	SE63	Slimbridge	15	SO70	
Ruswarp	41	NZ80	Selkirk	48	NT42	Slinfold	11	TQ13	
Rutherglen	47	NS66	Selly Oak	24	SP08	Slough	17	SU97	
Ruthin	29	SJ15	Selsey	11	SZ89	Smailholm	49	NT63	
Ruyton-XI-Towns	30	SJ32	Selstead	13	TR24	Small Dole	11	TQ21	
Ryde	10	SZ59	Senghenydd	14	ST19	Smallways	40	NZ11	
Rye	13	TQ92	Sennen	4	SW32	Smethwick	24	SP08	
Ryhope	45	NZ45	Sennybridge	22	SN92	Snainton	41	SE98	
Ryton	45	NZ16	Settle	39	SD86	Snaith	36	SE62	
			Sevenoaks	12	TQ55	Snape	19	TM35	
			Shaftesbury	11	ST82	Snarestone	31	SK30	
Sacriston	45	NZ24	Shaldon	8	SX97	Snetterton	27	TM08	
Sadberge	40	NZ31	Shalfleet	10	SZ48	Snettisham	26	TF63	
Saddell	46	NR73	Shandon	51	NS28	Snodland	12	TQ76	
Saffron Walden	18	TL53	Shanklin	10	SZ58	Solihull	24	SP17	
Salcombe Regis	8	SY18	Shap	39	NY51	Somerford	30	SJ86	
Salcombe	8	SX73	Shapwick	14	ST43	Somersham	26	TL37	
Sale	35	SJ79	Shardlow	31	SK43	Somerton	14	ST42	
Salen	54	NM66	Sharnbrook	25	SP95	Sonning	16	SU77	
Salford	35	SJ89	Sharnford	24	SP49	Sorbie	42	NX44	
Salhouse	27	TG3T	Sharpness	15	SO60	Sorisdale	50	NM26	
Saline	52	NT09	Shaw	35	SD90	Sorn	47	NS52	
Salisbury	10	SU12	Shawbury	30	SJ52	Soulby	39	NY71	
Saltash	5	SX45	Shawell	24	SP58	Sourton	5	SX58	
Saltburn-by-the-Sea	40	NZ62	Sheerness	13	TQ97	South Benfleet	18	TQ78	
Saltcoats	46	NS24	Sheerwater	17	TQ06	South Brent	8	SX66	
Saltfleet	37	TF49	Sheffield	31	SK38	South Godstone	12	TQ34	
Saltfleetby	37	TF49	Shefford	25	TL13	South Harting	11	SU71	
Salthouse	27	TG04	Sheldon	24	SP18	South Lopham	27	TM08	
Sampford Peverell	7	ST01	Shelf	35	SE12	South Milton	8	SX74	
Sandbach	30	SJ76	Shenstone	24	SK10	South Mimms	17	TL20	
Sandbanks	10	SZ08	Shepley	35	SE10	South Molton	6	SS72	
Sanderstead	12	TQ35	Shepperton	17	TQ06	South Normanton	31	SK45	
Sandford	14	ST45	Shepreth	18	TL34	South Ockendon	12	TQ58	
Sandgarth	67	HY51	Shepshed	32	SK41	South Otterington	40	SE38	
Sandhaven	63	NJ96	Shepton Mallet	15	ST64	South Petherton	9	ST41	
Sandhead	42	NX04	Sheraton	45	NZ43	South Queensferry	48	NT17	
Sandhurst	16	SU86	Sherborne	9	ST61	South Raynham	26	TF82	
Sandiacre	32	SK43	Sherburn	41	SE97	South Shields	45	NZ36	
Sandiway	30	SJ67	Sherburn-in-Elmet	36	SE43	South Walsham	27	TG31	
Sandness	63	HU15	Sherfield on Loddon	16	SU65	South Wigston	25	SP59	
Sandown	10	SZ58	Sheriff Hutton	40	SE66	South Witham	32	SK91	
Sandringham	26	TF62	Sheringham	27	TG14	South Woodham Ferrers	18	TQ89	
Sandsend	41	NZ81	Sherston	15	ST88	South Zeal	5	SX69	
Sandwich	13	TR35	Shevington	34	SD50	Southall	17	TQ18	
Sandy	25	TL14	Shieldaig	59	NG85	Southam	24	SP46	
Sandycroft	32	SJ36	Shifnal	30	SJ70	Southampton	10	SU41	
Sandygate	38	SC39	Shildon	40	NZ22	Southborough	12	TQ54	
Sanquhar	47	NS70	Shillingford	16	SU59	Southbourne	11	SU70	
Sarisbury	10	SU50	Shipdham	27	TF90	Southend-on-Sea	19	TQ88	
Sarn	28	SH23	Shipham	14	ST45	Southgate	17	TQ29	
Sarnesfield	23	SO35	Shiplake	16	SU77	Southminster	19	TQ99	
Sarre	13	TR26	Shipley	35	SE13	Southmoor	16	SU39	
Sartfield	38	SC39	Shipston-on-Stour	24	SP24	Southport	34	SD31	
Saughtree	44	NY59	Shipton-under-Wychwood	16	SP21	Southrepps	27	TG23	
Saul	15	SO70	Shiptonthorpe	36	SE84	Southsea	11	SZ69	
Saundersfoot	20	SN10	Shiremoor	45	NZ37	Southwell	32	SK75	
Saunderton	16	SP70	Shirley	24	SP17	Southwold	27	TM57	
Saunton	6	SS43	Shirrell Heath	10	SU51	Sowerby Bridge	35	SE02	
Sawbridgeworth	18	TL41	Shobdon	23	SO36	Sowton	8	SX99	
Sawston	18	TL44	Shoeburyness	19	TQ98	Spalding	33	TF22	

Place		
Sparkford	15	ST62
Spean Bridge	55	NN28
Speke	30	SJ48
Spencers Wood	16	SU76
Spennymoor	45	NZ23
Spey Bay	62	NJ36
Spilsby	33	TF46
Spratton	25	SP77
Springhead	35	SD90
Square and Compass	20	SN10
Stanton	26	TL97
St Abbs	49	NT96
St Agnes	4	SW75
St Albans	17	TL10
St Andrew	17	GN00
St Andrews	53	NO51
St Arvans	14	ST59
St Asaph	29	SJ07
St Aubin	9	JS00
St Austell	4	SX05
St Bees	38	NX91
St Blazey	5	SX05
St Boswells	48	NT53
St Brelade	9	JS00
St Brelade's Bay	9	JS00
St Brides	20	SM81
St Clears	20	SN21
St Cleer	5	SX26
St Clement's Bay	9	JS00
St Combs	63	NK06
St Cyrus	57	NO76
St David's	20	SN21
St Day	4	SW74
St Dogmael's	20	SN14
St Fergus	63	NK05
St Fillans	52	NN62
St Helens	34	SJ59
St Helens	11	SZ68
St Helier	9	JS00
St Ives	4	SW54
St Ives	26	TL37
St John	9	JS00
St John's Chapel	45	NY83
St John's	38	SC28
St Judes	38	SC49
St Just	4	SW33
St Keverne	4	SW72
St Lawrence	9	JS00
St Lawrence	10	SZ57
St Leonards	10	SU10
St Leonards-on-Sea	12	TO80
St Margaret's Hope	67	ND49
St Margarets Bay	13	TR34
St Mark's	38	SC37
St Martin	9	GN00
St Martin	9	JS00
St Mary Church	7	ST07
St Mary's	9	JS00
St Mary's Bay	13	TR02
St Marychurch	8	SX96
St Marys	67	HY40
St Mawes	4	SW83
St Mawgan	4	SW86
St Mellion	5	SX36
St Michael's on Wyre	34	SD44
St Monans	53	NO50
St Neot	5	SX16
St Neots	25	TL16
St Nicholas at Wade	13	TR26
St Ouen	9	JS00
St Peter	9	JS00
St Peter Port	9	GN00
St Sampson	9	GN00
St Saviour	9	JS00
St Teath	5	SX08
St Wenn	4	SW96
Stadhampton	16	SU69
Staffin	58	NG46
Stafford	30	SJ92
Staindrop	40	NZ12
Staines	17	TQ07
Stainforth	39	SD86
Staithes	41	NZ71
Statham	27	TG32
Stalybridge	35	SJ99
Stamford Bridge	41	SE75
Stamford	33	TF00
Standish	34	SD51
Standlake	16	SP30
Stanhope	45	NY93
Stanley	52	NO13
Stanley	45	NZ15
Stanmore	17	TQl9
Stansted	18	TL52
Stanstead Abbotts	18	TL31
Stanton Harcourt	16	SP40
Stanton	27	TL97
Stanway	8	SP03
Stapleford	32	SK43
Staplehurst	12	TQ74
Starcross	8	SX98
Starkigarth	63	HU42
Staunton	23	SO51
Staveley	31	SK47
Staverton	8	SX76
Staxton	41	TA07
Steeple Aston	24	SP42
Steeple Bumpstead	18	TL64
Steeton	35	SE04
Stein	58	NG25
Stelling Minnis	13	TR14
Stepaside	20	SN10
Stepps	47	NS66
Stevenage	17	TL22
Stevenston	24	NS24
Stewarton	47	NS44
Stibb Cross	6	SS41
Stickney	33	TF35
Stilligarry	64	NF73
Stillington	40	SE56
Stilton	25	TL18
Stirling	52	NS79
Stockbridge	10	SU33
Stockport	35	SJ88
Stocksbridge	35	SK29
Stockton Heath	30	SJ68
Stockton-on-Tees	40	NZ41
Stoer	64	NC02
Stogursey	14	ST24
Stoke Canon	8	SX99
Stoke Ferry	26	TF70
Stoke Fleming	8	SX84
Stoke Gabriel	8	SX85
Stoke Goldington	25	SP84
Stoke Holy Cross	27	TG20
Stoke Mandeville	16	SP81
Stoke-by-Nayland	19	TL93
Stoke-on-Trent	30	SJ84
Stokenchurch	16	SU79
Stokesley	40	NZ50
Ston Easton	15	ST65
Stone	30	SJ93
Stonehaven	57	NO88
Stonehouse	15	SO80
Stoneykirk	42	NX05
Stonor	16	SU78
Stornoway	64	NB43
Storrington	11	TQ01
Stotfold	18	TL23
Stourbridge	24	SO98
Stourport-on-Severn	23	SO87
Stourton	23	SO88
Stow Cum Quy	18	TL56
Stow	48	NT44
Stow Bedon	27	TL99
Stow-on-the-Wold	24	SP12
Stowmarket	19	TM05
Strachan	57	NO69
Strachur	51	NN00
Stradbroke	27	TM27
Stradishall	18	TL75
Stradsett	26	TF60
Straiton	47	NS30
Stranraer	42	NX06
Stratfield Turgis	16	SU65
Stratford	18	TQ38
Stratford-upon-Avon	24	SP25
Strathkanaird	65	NC10
Strathaven	47	NS74
Strathblane	52	NS57
Strathcarron	59	NG94
Strathdon	57	NJ31
Strathmiglo	53	NO21
Strathpeffer	60	NH45
Strathy	66	NC86
Strathyre	52	NN51
Stratton	6	SS20
Streatham	17	TQ27
Streatley	16	SU58
Street	14	ST43
Streetly	24	SP09
Strensall	40	SE66
Strete	8	SX84
Stretford	35	SJ79
Stretham	26	TL57
Stretton	30	SJ68
Stretton	32	SK91
Strichen	63	NJ95
Stromeferry	59	NG83
Stromness	67	HY20
Stronachlachar	51	NN41
Strone	51	NS18
Strontian	54	NM86
Strood	12	TQ76
Stroud	15	SO80
Struan	58	NG33
Struy	60	NH43
Studland	10	SZ08
Studley	24	SP06
Sturminster Newton	9	ST71
Sturton	32	SK88
Sudbury	31	SK13
Sudbury	19	TL84
Sulby	38	SC39
Sullom Voe	63	HU47
Sumburgh	63	HU40
Summercourt	4	SW85
Sunbury-on-Thames	17	TQ16
Sunderland	45	NZ35
Surbiton	17	TQ16
Sutterton	33	TF23
Sutton Benger	15	ST97
Sutton Coldfield	24	SP19
Sutton Scotney	10	SU43
Sutton	12	TQ26
Sutton Veny	15	ST84
Sutton upon Derwent	36	SE74
Sutton Valence	12	TO84
Sutton-in-Ashfield	32	SK45
Sutton in the Elms	24	SP59
Sutton-on-Sea	33	TF58
Sutton-on-the-Forest	40	SE56
Sutton-on-Trent	32	SK76
Swadlincote	31	SK31
Swaffham	26	TF80
Swainswick	15	ST76
Swalcliffe	24	SP33
Swallowfield	16	SU76
Swanage	10	SZ07
Swanley	12	TQ56
Swansea	21	SS69
Sway	10	SZ29
Swaythling	10	SU41
Swillington	36	SE33
Swindon	15	SU18
Swineshead	33	TF24
Swineshead	25	TL06
Swinton	9	NT84
Swinton	36	SK49
Swinton	26	TF83
Syderstone	26	TF83
Symbister	63	HU56
Symington	44	NS93
Symonds Yat	23	SO51
Synod	21	SN45
Syre	66	NC64
Syston	32	SK61
Tadcaster	36	SE44
Tadley	16	SU56
Tadworth	12	TQ25
Taff's Well	14	ST18
Tain	61	NH78
Tal-y-Bont	28	SH76
Tal-y-Bont	29	SH77
Tal-y-Llyn	28	SH70
Talgarreg	21	SN45
Talgarth	22	SO13
Talladale	59	NG97
Talland Bay	5	SX25
Talsarnau	28	SH63
Talybont	22	SN68
Talybont-on-Usk	22	SO12
Tamworth	25	SK20
Tan-y-Groes	20	SN24
Tangmere	11	SU90
Tangusdale	64	NF60
Tankerton	13	TR16
Tannadice	53	NO45
Taplow	16	SU98
Tarbert	58	NB10
Tarbert	51	NR86
Tarbet	51	NN30
Tarbolton	47	NS42
Tarfside	57	NO47
Tarland	57	NJ40
Tarleton	34	SD42
Tarporley	30	SJ56
Tarrant Keyneston	9	ST90
Tarskavaig	58	NG50
Tarves	22	NJ83
Taunton Deane S A	7	ST12
Taunton	14	ST22
Tavistock	5	SX47
Tayinloan	46	NR74
Taynuilt	55	NN03
Tayport	53	NO42
Tayvallich	50	NR78
Teangue	56	NG60
Tedburn St Mary	8	SX89
Teddington	17	TQ17
Teesside Airport	40	NZ31
Teignmouth	8	SX97
Telford	30	SJ60
Temple Bar	21	SN55
Temple Ewell	13	TR24
Temple	48	NT35
Temple Sowerby	39	NY62
Templecombe	15	ST72
Templeton	22	SN11
Tenbury Wells	23	SO56
Tenby	20	SN10
Tenterden	13	TQ83
Tern Hill	30	SJ63
Tetbury	15	ST89
Tetford	33	TF37
Teviothead	44	NT40
Tewkesbury	23	SO83
Thakeham	11	TQ11
Thame	16	SP70
Thames Ditton	17	TQ16
Thatcham	16	SU56

Place	No.	Grid
Thaxted	18	TL63
The Barringtons	24	SP21
The Bungalow	38	SC38
The Lhen	38	NX30
Theale	16	SU67
Thetford	26	TL88
Theydon Bois	18	TQ49
Thirlspot	38	NY31
Thirsk	40	SE48
Thornaby	40	NZ41
Thornbury	15	ST69
Thorne	36	SE61
Thorney	26	TF20
Thorngumbald	37	TA22
Thornhill	52	NS69
Thornhill	43	NX89
Thornley	45	NZ33
Thornthwaite	38	NY22
Thornton Dale	41	SE88
Thornton Heath	17	TQ36
Thornton Hough	29	SJ38
Thornton	34	SD30
Thornton	34	SD34
Thornton Watlass	40	SE28
Thornton-le-Street	40	SE48
Thorpe Bay	13	TQ98
Thorpe Market	27	TG23
Thorpe	31	SK15
Thorpe Thewles	40	NZ32
Thorpe-le-Soken	19	TM12
Thorpeness	19	TM45
Thorverton	7	SS90
Thrapston	25	SP97
Three Cocks	22	SO13
Three Legged Cross	10	SU00
Threekingham	33	TF03
Threlkeld	38	NY32
Threshfield	39	SD96
Thropton	45	NU00
Throwleigh	5	SX69
Thrumster	67	ND34
Thrussington	32	SK61
Thurcroft	36	SK48
Thurlaston	24	SP47
Thurlestone	5	SX64
Thurmaston	32	SK60
Thurnby	25	SK60
Thurnscoe	36	SE40
Thursby	44	NY35
Thurso	67	ND16
Thwaite	39	SD89
Tickenham	14	ST47
Tickhill	36	SK59
Ticknall	31	SK32
Tideford	5	SX35
Tideswell	31	SK17
Tigharry	64	NF77
Tighnabruaich	51	NR97
Tilbury	12	TQ67
Tilford	11	SU84
Tillicoultry	52	NS99
Tilshead	15	SU04
Tilton	32	SK70
Timperley	35	SJ78
Tintagel	5	SX08
Tintern	14	SO50
Tintinhull	9	ST41
Tintwistle	35	SK09
Tipton	24	SO99
Tiptree	19	TL81
Titchwell	26	TF74
Tiverton	7	SS91
Tividale	24	SO99
Tobermory	54	NM55
Tockwith	36	SE45
Toddington	25	TL02
Todmorden	35	SD92
Todwick	32	SK48
Tollesbury	19	TL91
Tolleshunt D'Arcy	19	TL91
Tolworth	17	TQ16
Tomatin	61	NH72
Tomdoun	55	NH10
Tomich	60	NH32
Tomintoul	56	NJ11
Tommavoulin	61	NJ22
Ton Pentre	21	SS99
Tonbridge	12	TQ54
Tongue	66	NC55
Tonypandy	14	SS99
Tonyrefail	14	ST08
Topcliffe	40	SE47
Topsham	8	SX98
Torcross	8	SX84
Tore	60	NH55
Tormarton	15	ST77
Torness	60	NH52
Torphins	57	NJ60
Torpoint	5	SX45
Torquay	8	SX96
Torrance	47	NS67
Torridon	59	NG95
Torrin	58	NG52
Torthorwald	43	NY07
Torver	38	SD29
Totland Bay	10	SZ38
Totnes	8	SX86
Tottington	35	SD71
Totton	10	SU31
Tow Law	45	NZ13
Towcester	25	SP64
Traethsaith	20	SN25
Tranent	48	NT47
Tranmere	29	SJ38
Traquair	48	NT33
Trawsfynydd	28	SH73
Trearddur Bay	28	SH27
Trebetherick	4	SW97
Trecastle	22	SN82
Tredegar	14	SO10
Treekingham	32	TF03
Trefriw	29	SH76
Tregaron	21	SN65
Tregony	4	SW94
Treherbert	21	SS99
Trelleck	14	SO50
Tremadog	28	SH54
Treorchy	14	SS99
Trevor	29	SJ24
Treyarnon Bay	4	SW87
Trimdon	45	NZ33
Trimingham	27	TG23
Tring	17	SP91
Trinity	9	JS00
Troon	47	NS33
Trotton	11	SU82
Troutbeck	39	NY40
Trowbridge	15	ST85
Truro	4	SW84
Tummel Bridge	52	NN75
Tunbridge Wells	12	TQ53
Tunstall	19	TM35
Turnberry	46	NS20
Turners Hill	12	TQ33
Turriff	62	NJ74
Turton	35	SD71
Turney	25	SP95
Tutbury	31	SK22
Tuxford	32	SK77
Twatt	67	HY22
Tweedsmuir	48	NT02
Twickenham	17	TQ17
Two Bridges	5	SX67
Twycross	31	SK30
Twyford	10	SU42
Twyford	16	SU77
Tyldesley	34	SD60
Tyn-y-Cefn	29	SJ04
Tyndrum	55	NN33
Tynemouth	45	NZ36
Tynet	62	NJ36
Tywyn	22	SH50
Ubley	14	ST55
Uckfield	12	TQ42
Uddingston	47	NS66
Uffculme	7	ST01
Uffington	30	SJ51
Uig	64	NB03
Uig	58	NG36
Ulceby	33	TF47
Uldale	44	NY23
Ullapool	65	NH19
Ullesthorpe	24	SP58
Ulpha	38	SD19
Ulsta	63	HU47
Ulverston	38	SD27
Umberleigh	6	SS62
Unapool	65	NC23
Union Mills	38	SC37
Upavon	15	SU15
Upermill	35	SD90
Uphall	48	NT07
Upholland	34	SD50
Upminster	18	TQ58
Upottery	8	ST20
Upper Gronant	29	SJ18
Upper Largo	53	NO40
Upper Slaughter	24	SP12
Uppingham	25	SP89
Upton	36	SE41
Upton upon Severn	23	SO84
Urmston	35	SJ79
Usk	14	SO30
Uttoxeter	31	SK03
Uxbridge	17	TQ08
Vale	9	GN00
Valley	28	SH27
Ventnor	10	SZ57
Verwood	10	SU00
Veryan	4	SW93
Vickerstown	38	SD16
Virkie	63	HU31
Voe	63	HU46
Waddington	35	SD74
Waddington	32	SK96
Wadebridge	4	SW97
Wadhurst	12	TQ63
Wainfleet	33	TF45
Wakefield	35	SE32
Walkden	35	SD70
Walkerburn	48	NT33
Walkington	37	SE93
Wall	45	NY96
Wallasey	34	SJ29
Wallingford	16	SU68
Wallington	17	TQ26
Walls	63	HU24
Wallsend	45	NZ26
Wallyford	48	NT37
Walmer	13	TR35
Walsall	24	SP09
Walsden	35	SD92
Waltham Abbey	18	TL30
Waltham Cross	17	TL30
Waltham	37	TA20
Waltham-on-the-Wolds	32	SK82
Walthamstow	17	TQ38
Walton	23	SO25
Walton-on-Thames	17	TQ16
Walton-on-the-Naze	19	TM22
Wamphray	43	NY19
Wandsworth	17	TQ27
Wanlockhead	47	NS81
Wansford	25	TL09
Wantage	16	SU48
Warboys	26	TL38
Warburton	34	SJ78
Warcop	39	NY71
Ware	17	TL31
Wareham	9	SY98
Wargrave	16	SU77
Wark	44	NY87
Warkworth	45	NU20
Warmington	24	SP44
Warminster	15	ST84
Warmley	15	ST67
Warmsworth	36	SE50
Warrington	34	SJ68
Warsash	10	SU40
Warsop	32	SK56
Warton	34	SD42
Warwick	24	SP26
Wasbister	67	HY33
Wasdale Head	38	NY10
Wasdale	38	NY10
Washingborough	32	TF07
Washington	45	NZ35
Watchet	7	ST04
Waterbeach	11	SU80
Watergate Bay	4	SW86
Wateringbury	12	TQ65
Waterlooville	11	SU60
Watermillock	39	NY42
Waterrow	7	ST02
Watford	17	TQ19
Wath-upon-Dearne	36	SE40
Watlington	16	SU69
Watnall	32	SK44
Watten	67	ND25
Watton	26	TF90
Watton-at-Stone	17	TL21
Wealdstone	17	TQ18
Weare	14	ST45
Wearhead	44	NY83
Weaverham	30	SJ67
Wedmore	14	ST44
Wednesbury	24	SO99
Wednesfield	24	SJ90
Weedon	25	SP65
Weldon	25	SP98
Welford	25	SP68
Wellesbourne	24	SP25
Welling	12	TQ47
Wellingborough	25	SP86
Wellington	30	SJ61
Wellington	7	ST12
Wells	14	ST54
Wells-next-the-Sea	26	TF94
Welney	26	TL59
Welshampton	30	SJ43
Welshpool	29	SJ20
Welwyn Garden City	17	TL21
Wem	30	SJ52
Wembley	17	TQ18
Wembury	5	SX54
Wemyss Bay	51	NS16
Wendover	16	SP80
Wensley	40	SE08
Wentbridge	36	SE41
Weobley	23	SO45
West Aukland	40	NZ12
West Bergholt	19	TL92
West Bexington	9	SY58
West Bilney	26	TF71
West Bromwich	24	SP09
West Byfleet	17	TQ06
West Calder	48	NT06

West Chiltington

West Chiltington	11	TQ01
West Coker	9	ST51
West Drayton	17	TQ07
West Haddon	25	SP67
West Harptree	14	ST55
West Horsley	11	TQ05
West Kilbride	46	NS24
West Kirby	29	SJ28
West Lavington	15	SU05
West Linton	48	NT15
West Lulworth	9	SY88
West Meon	11	SU62
West Mersea	19	TM01
West Molesey	17	TQ16
West Pentire	4	SW76
West Quantoxhead	7	ST14
West Runton	27	TG14
West Thurrock	12	TQ57
West Wellow	10	SU21
West Wickham	12	TQ36
West Wittering	11	SZ79
West Witton	40	SE08
West Woodburn	45	NY88
Westbury	30	SJ30
Westbury	15	ST85
Westbury-upon-Severn	23	SO71
Westcliff-on-Sea	12	TQ88
Westerdale	12	ND15
Westerham	12	TQ45
Westgate-on-Sea	13	TR37
Westhill	57	NJ80
Westhoughton	34	SD60
Westleton	19	TM46
Weston	18	TL23
Weston	30	SJ52
Weston	31	SJ92
Weston-Super-Mare	14	ST36
Weston-in-Gordano	14	ST47
Weston-on-the-Green	16	SP51
Weston-under-Lizard	30	SJ81
Westonbirt	15	ST88
Westward Ho!	6	SS42
Wetheral	44	NY45
Wetherby	36	SE44
Wethersfield	18	TL73
Weybourne	27	TG14
Weybridge	17	TQ06
Weymouth	9	SY67
Whaley Bridge	31	SK08
Whalley	35	SD73
Whauphill	42	NX44
Wheathampstead	17	TL11
Wheatley	16	SP50
Wheddon Cross	7	SS93
Whickham	45	NZ26
Whiddon Down	5	SX49
Whimple	8	SY09
Whippingham	10	SZ59
Whipsnade	17	TL01
Whitburn	47	NS96
Whitburn	45	NZ46
Whitby	41	NZ81
Whitchurch	30	SJ54
Whitchurch	23	SO51
Whitchurch	16	SP82
Whitchurch	10	SU44
Whitebridge	60	NH41
Whitebrook	14	SO50
Whitefield	35	SD80
Whitehall	67	HY62
Whitehaven	38	NX91
Whitehills	62	NJ66
Whitemoor	4	SW95
Whiteness	63	HU34
Whitestone	23	SO54
Whithorn	42	NX44
Whiting Bay	46	NS02
Whitland	20	SN21
Whitley Bay	45	NZ37
Whitney-on-Wye	23	SO24
Whitstable	13	TR16
Whittington	29	SJ33
Whittle le Woods	34	SD52
Whittlesey	26	TL29
Whitton	23	SO26
Whitwell	10	SZ57
Whitwell-on-the-Hill	41	SE76
Whitworth	35	SD81
Wick	67	ND35
Wickersley	36	SK49
Wickford	18	TQ79
Wickham Market	19	TM35
Wickham	10	SU51
Wickwar	15	ST78
Widdrington	45	NZ29
Widecombe in the Moor	8	SX77
Widemouth Bay	6	SS20
Widmerpool	32	SK62
Widnes	30	SJ58
Wigan	34	SD50
Wigston	25	SP69
Wigton	44	NY24
Wigtown	42	NX45
Wilkieston	48	NT16
Willenhall	24	SO99
Willerby	37	TA03
Willersey	24	SP13
Willersley	23	SO34
Willingham	26	TL47
Willington	45	NZ13
Williton	7	ST04
Wilmcote	24	SP15
Wilmington	8	SY29
Wilmslow	30	SJ88
Wilsontown	47	NS95
Wilton	15	SU03
Wimbledon	17	TQ27
Wimborne Minster	10	SZO9
Wincanton	15	ST72
Winchelsea	13	TQ91
Winchester	10	SU42
Windermere	39	SD49
Windsor	17	SU97
Wing	16	SP82
Wingham	13	TR25
Winkleigh	6	SS60
Winnard's Perch	4	SW96
Winnersh	16	SU77
Winscombe	14	ST45
Winsford	30	SJ66
Winsford	7	SS93
Winslow	25	SP72
Winston	40	NZ11
Winterbourne	15	ST68
Winterbourne Abbas	9	SY69
Winterbourne Whitechurch	9	ST80
Winterton-on-Sea	27	TG41
Wirksworth	31	SK25
Wisbech	33	TF40
Wishaw	47	NS75
Wishaw	24	SP19
Witham	18	TL81
Withern	33	TF48
Withernsea	37	TA32
Witherslack	39	SD48
Withleigh	7	SS91
Withybrook	24	SP48
Withypool	7	SS83
Witney	16	SP30
Witton-le-Wear	45	NZ13
Wiveliscombe	7	ST02
Wix	19	TM12
Woburn	25	SP93
Woburn Sands	25	SP93
Woking	17	TQ05
Wokingham	16	SU86
Wolsingham	45	NZ03
Wolverhampton	24	SO99
Wolviston	40	NZ42
Wombwell	36	SE30
Wooburn Common	16	SU98
Wooburn Green	16	SU98
Woodbridge	19	TM24
Woodchurch	13	TQ93
Woodford Green	18	TQ39
Woodhall Spa	33	TF16
Woodhead	35	SK09
Woodingdean	12	TQ30
Woodlands	36	SE50
Woodlands	10	SU31
Woodstock	16	SP41
Woodville	31	SK31
Woody Bay	6	SS64
Woofferton	23	SO56
Wool	9	SY88
Woolacombe	6	SS44
Wooler	49	NT92
Woolfardisworthy	6	SS32
Woolmer Green	18	TL21
Woolverton	15	ST75
Woore	30	SJ74
Wootton Bassett	15	SU08
Wootton Bridge	10	SZ59
Wootton	10	SZ59
Wootton	13	TR24
Wootton	37	TA10
Worcester	23	SO85
Worcester Park	17	TQ26
Worfield	23	SO79
Workington	38	NX92
Worksop	32	SK57
Wormit	53	NO32
Worplesdon	17	SU95
Worsley	35	SD70
Worthing	11	TQ10
Wortley	35	SK39
Wortwell	27	TM28
Wotton-under-Edge	15	ST79
Wragby	33	TF17
Wrangaton	8	SX65
Wrangle	33	TF45
Wrea Green	34	SD33
Wrelton	41	SE78
Wrentham	27	TM48
Wrexham	29	SJ35
Wrightington Bar	34	SD51
Writtle	18	TL60
Wrotham Heath	12	TQ65

Zennor

Wroxall	10	SZ58
Wroxham	27	TG21
Wroxton	24	SP44
Wychbold	24	SO96
Wykeham	41	SE98
Wymondham	32	SK81
Wymondham	27	TG10
Yalding	12	TQ64
Yarcombe	8	ST20
Yardley Hastings	25	SP85
Yarm	40	NZ41
Yarrow	48	NT32
Yate	15	ST78
Yateley	16	SU86
Yattendon	16	SU57
Yatton Keynell	15	ST87
Yaxley	27	TM17
Yeadon	35	SE24
Yealmpton	5	SX55
Yelland	6	SS43
Yelverton	5	SX56
Yelverton	27	TG20
Yeovil	9	ST51
Yetholm	49	NT82
Yetts O'Muckhart	52	NO00
York	36	SE65
Youlgrave	31	SK26
Yoxall	31	SK11
Yoxford	19	TM36
Ysbyty Ystwyth	22	SN77
Ystalyfera	21	SN70
Ystrad Mynach	14	ST19
Ystradgynlais	21	SN71
Zeals	15	ST73
Zelah	4	SW85
Zennor	4	SW43